lonely planet

POCKET

DELHI & AGRA

TOP SIGHTS · LOCAL EXPERIENCES

DANIEL MCCROHAN
BRADLEY MAYHEW

Contents

Plan Your Trip   4

Akbar's Mausoleum, Sikandra (p131)
ZORAN KARAPANCEV/SHUTTERSTOCK ©

Welcome to Delhi & Agra

It's no shock that Mughal India's two great capital cities flaunt such incredible historical riches – not least the peerless Taj Mahal – but Delhi and Agra spring some surprises too. Heavenly street food, gloriously chaotic bazaars and, in Delhi's modern suburbs, sky trains that zip shoppers from mall to mall, offer a tantalising glimpse of the India of the future.

Qutab Minar (p109)
AVIGATOR FORTUNER/SHUTTERSTOCK

Top Sights

Taj Mahal

The ultimate monument to love. **p122**

OLENA TUR/SHUTTERSTOCK ©

SUMIT KUMAR 09/SHUTTERSTOCK ©

Qutab Minar Complex

The world's tallest brick minaret. **p108**

ROOP_DEY/SHUTTERSTOCK ©

Agra Fort

Awesome red-sandstone riverside fortress. **p126**

RAVI KRISHNAN GUPTA/SHUTTERSTOCK ©

Mehrauli Archaeological Park

Forested park scattered with ruins. **p110**

Humayun's Tomb

Inspiration for the Taj Mahal. **p78**

Red Fort

Old Delhi's immense Mughal fortress. **p34**

Hazrat Nizam-ud-din Dargah

Spiritual, atmospheric shrine. **p80**

Rajpath

Parade grounds of the British Raj. **p58**

Purana Qila
Delhi's prodigious 'Old Fort'. **p76**

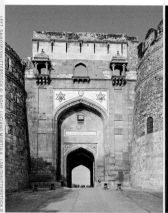

Jama Masjid
Delhi's principal mosque. **p38**

Fatehpur Sikri
Emperor Akbar's ghostly abandoned city. **p136**

Akshardham Temple
Delhi's largest Hindu temple. **p92**

Eating

While Delhiites graze all day on the city's masterful, taste-tingling Dilli-ka-Chaat, *the city's dining scene is also becoming increasingly diverse. Creative cuisine at Delhi's modern restaurants now sits alongside traditional purveyors of delicate dhals and meaty Mughal delights. In Agra, fans of street food should make a beeline for* chaat galli *(snack alley).*

Dilli-ka-Chaat

Old Delhi sizzles with the sound of *Dilli-ka-Chaat* (street-food snacks) being fried, boiled, grilled and flipped. *Chaat* to look out for include: *dahi bhalle* (fried lentil balls served with yoghurt and garnished with chutney); *aloo tikki* (spiced potato patties; pictured above); *shakarkandi* (sweet potato) baked on coals on a flip-out table; and *aloo chaat* (fried pieces of par-boiled potato mixed with chickpeas and chopped onions, and garnished with spices and chutney).

Breakfast in Delhi

Aside from *Dilli-ka-Chaat*, Delhi specialities include breakfast-favourite *chole bhature* (spicy chickpeas, accompanied by puffy, fried bread with a light paneer filling); and *chole kulche*, a healthier version of *chole bhature* made with boiled chickpeas and less-greasy baked bread. *Nihari* (goat curry eaten with roti) is a popular breakfast for Delhi's Muslim population, and the only breakfast item at legendary Karim's (p46).

Street Sweets

Devilishly sticky *jalebi* (orange-coloured coils of deep-fried batter dunked in sugar syrup) are served hot from numerous holes-in-the-wall across the city; Old Delhi's Jalebi Wala (p47) is the most famous of the lot.

Those with a sweet tooth should also seek out one of the old *kheer* (rice pudding) makers, and on a hot day you can do no wrong with a *kulfi* (traditional Indian ice cream), while some Old Delhi lemon-drink sellers still serve handmade lemonade

MRINALPAL/SHUTTERSTOCK ©

from glass bottles sealed with a marble.

Best Budget Eats

Darbar Setting the bar for budget food in Paharganj, this all-veg restaurant isn't dirt cheap, but is fabulously good value. (p48)

Sita Ram Dewan Chand The capital's most famous supplier of Delhi's go-to breakfast choice: *chole bhature.* (p48)

Tadka An all-veg Indian restaurant that's a notch above its Main Bazaar competitors. (p49)

Andhra Pradesh Bhawan Canteen Expect long queues and table-sharing;

that's what you get when food is this good, and this cheap. (p67)

Best Midrange Eats

Karim's Much loved by Delhi's Muslim population, legendary Karim's serves unrivalled goat, lamb and flatbreads. (p46)

Mama Chicken Agra's superstar *dhaba* (casual eatery) with duelling veg and nonveg glorified street stalls that employ 24 cooks during the rush. (p131)

Naivedyam South Indian restaurant with an exquisite temple-like interior. (p101)

Best Fine Dining

Indian Accent Five-star restaurant serving contemporary Indian cuisine from the grounds of luxury Lodhi hotel. (p85)

Esphahan Agra's finest restaurant in its finest hotel offers an exquisite menu chock-full of unique delicacies, but anything that comes out of the succulent North Indian tandoor is a showstopper. (p132)

Lakhori Mughlai delights in the courtyard restaurant of the charming Old Delhi hotel, Haveli Dharampura. (p48)

Old Delhi's Delicious Street Food

JAYANT BAHEL/SHUTTERSTOCK ©

Dilli-ka-Chaat Favourites

○ *chole bhature* – spicy chickpeas, accompanied by puffy, fried bread with a light paneer filling; a breakfast favourite

○ *dahi bhalle* – fried lentil balls served with yoghurt and chutney

○ *aloo tikki* – spiced potato patties

○ *jalebi* – orange-coloured coils of deep-fried batter dunked in sugar syrup

○ *kheer* – rice pudding

★ Top Places for Delhi Street Food

Sita Ram Dewan Chand (p48) A hole-in-the-wall serving inexpensive portions of just one dish – *chhole bhature*.

Natraj Dahi Balle Corner (p46) This tiny place is famous for its *dahi bhalle* and deliciously crispy *aloo tikki*.

Jalebi Wala (p47) Century-old Jalebi Wala does Delhi's finest *jalebis*.

PT Gaya Prasad Shiv Charan (p47) This is the most popular *paratha* joint in Old Delhi.

Bade Mia Ki Kheer (p47) Family owned, serving superdelicious, creamy, cardamon-scented *kheer*.

Standing Room Only

Old Delhi is the place to come for your *Dilli-ka-Chaat* (street-food snacks). Most places are simple street-side stalls or hole-in-the-wall joints with nowhere to sit, but sometimes a couple of tables to stand beside. There's rarely any menu as most places tend only to sell one or two items, which you can easily just point at to order. If in doubt, just have whatever the person next to you has ordered. It's bound to be tasty.

Sweet *jalebi*

PRAVIN SONI/SHUTTERSTOCK ©

Drinking & Nightlife

Delhi's ever-growing cafe scene has given rise to artisanal coffee, while the city's bar and live-music choices are also burgeoning. For the latest places to go at night, check out Little Black Book (https://lbb.in/delhi) or Brown Paper Bag (http://brownpaperbag.in/delhi). For drinks in Agra, seek out a hotel rooftop restaurant.

Bars

Delhi's nightlife is very quiet when compared with similar sized cities in the West, but there are a few decent bars, some with live music, dotted across the South Delhi enclaves. In the centre, there are some cocktail and single-malt hangouts in five-star hotels, while bars in Connaught Place tend to be brash and a bit samey, with a few exceptions. Backpacker-centred Paharganj has some dives that are fun hangouts, with reasonably cheap beer.

A smart-casual dress code (no shorts, vests or flip-flops) applies at many places. Many bars have two-for-one happy hours from around noon till 8pm.

Alcohol-free nightlife

There are ubiquitous coffee chains, including Café Coffee Day, Costa and Starbucks, but Delhi also has independent cafes that are doing special things, with fine fresh-grind coffees and organic eats.

Many locals and domestic tourists, especially families, spend the evening enjoying a stroll along night-time promenades such as Rajpath or Connaught Place, buying *Dilli-ka-Chaat* and ice cream from pop-up stalls. Some street markets, such as Paharganj's Main Bazaar, stay open after dark, and are buzzing places to go for an evening stroll even if you're not intent on actually buying anything.

Best Bars

Unplugged A step up from the usual Connaught Place drinking dross, Unplugged offers live music and tables

JEREMY SUTTON-HIBBERT/ALAMY ©

under a huge banyan tree. (p70)

Piano Man Jazz Club A funky, dim-lit speakeasy with the best live jazz in Delhi. (p103)

Hauz Khas Social Hauz Khas's hippest bar has craft beer, cocktails and a friendly vibe. (p103)

Ek Bar Stylish bar with some serious mixology. (p104)

1911 Sip the perfect cocktail against a backdrop of maharaja murals in the Imperial's classiest bar. (pictured above; p69)

Sam's Bar The most laid-back dive bar in Paharganj. (p52)

Best for Coffee

Blue Tokai Delhi's premier coffee roaster is hidden in the cool-as-cats art enclave of Champa Gali. (p117)

Ama Popular cafe with good food and strong coffee in the heart of Delhi's Tibetan community. (p50)

Triveni Terrace Cafe French-press coffee overlooking an art gallery's open-air amphitheatre. (p68)

Kunzum Travel Cafe Super laid-back cafe with a pay-what-you-like policy. (p104)

Indian Coffee House Dirt-cheap South Indian filter coffee served by waiters in fan-tailed hats. (p70)

Best for Tea

Jugmug Thela Aromatic brews, plus very unusual sandwiches, in this marvellous tea specialist in Champa Gali art enclave. (p118)

Chai Point Funky Connaught Place cafe specialising in healthy chai infusions (masala, cardamom, lemon grass). (p70)

Cha Bar Oxford Bookstore's buzzing cafe has more than 150 types of tea to choose from. (p70)

Atrium Is there anything more genteel than high tea at the Imperial? (p70)

Shopping & Markets

Wares from all over India glitter in Delhi's emporiums, markets and medieval bazaars. The city is also increasingly a centre of contemporary design, with independent boutiques and big shiny malls. Agra is well known for its marble items inlaid with coloured stones, similar to the pietra dura work on the Taj.

Markets

The lifeblood of Delhi's shopping scene, street-market bazaars are what make this city so wonderfully enchanting. Old Delhi is the hub of this traditional commercial world, and losing yourself, and your bearings, in its back-alley bazaars will rank high in your favourite Delhi memories. Things to seek out include silk saris, jootis (leather slippers), embroidery, metalwork, electronics, bangles and other jewellery, and a seemingly endless amount of clothing.

Many of the narrow-lane bazaars fan off Chandni Chowk, itself a busy, traffic-clogged market street, while a short walk north is the world's second-largest spice market. Not far away, Paharganj's backpacker-hub Main Bazaar is great for souvenirs, and nearby Connaught Place has large handicrafts emporiums that are perfect for a last-minute souvenir dash.

Further afield in South Delhi, you'll find higher-class markets such as Khan Market, Hauz Khas and Shahpur Jat Village with coffee shops and restaurants alongside trendy boutiques.

In Agra, the narrow streets behind Jama Masjid are a crazy maze of overcrowded lanes bursting with colourful markets.

Best Markets

Kinari Bazaar Extremely photogenic, Kinari is famous for *zardozi* (gold embroidery), temple trim and wedding turbans. (p52)

Ballimaran Specialises in sequined slippers and fancy, curly-toed jootis. (p53)

Spice Market Pinch your nose to stop yourself sneezing, then wander past fragrant mountains of turmeric powder and chillies. (p53)

ALMAZOFF/SHUTTERSTOCK ©

Main Bazaar Paharganj's backpacker hub sells tourist trinkets and clothes galore. (p54)

Majnu-ka-Tilla Delhi's Tibetan market; fascinating tangle of alleyways selling all manner of Tibetan trinkets. (p50)

Nai Sarak Old Delhi bazaar lined with stalls selling saris, shawls, chiffon and *lehenga* (blouse and skirt combo). (p53)

Khan Market Upmarket clothing and accessories shops, plus tons of restaurants, in a surprisingly ramshackle cluster. (p88)

Hauz Khas Tuck into trendy top-end clothing boutiques (pictured above) before your side dish of 14th-century Lodi-era ruins. (p104)

Best for Clothing

Fabindia Exquisite cotton and silk Indian clothing at very reasonable prices; branches all over town. (p72)

Khadi Gramodyog Bhawan Great-value Indian clothing made from the *khadi* (homespun cotton) famously championed by Gandhi. (p73)

Shahpur Jat Village High-quality clothing boutiques in an arty suburban village. (p105)

Hauz Khas Browse through an array of trendy boutiques then dive into the cafes, bars and restaurants. (p104)

NeedleDust Elegant embroidered jootis. (p105)

Best for Souvenirs

Central Cottage Industries Emporium India-wide clothing and handicrafts all under one roof; ideal for a final-day souvenir binge. (p71)

State Emporiums Collection of regional souvenir shops in one handy stretch near Connaught Place. (p73)

Main Bazaar Backpacker-favourite street market selling every India souvenir you'd ever want – plus plenty you don't. (p54)

Kamala Crafts, curios, textiles and homewares from the Crafts Council of India. (p71)

Subhash Emporium Agra's most-renowned marble shop. (p135)

Spiritual Delhi & Agra

Religion plays a key role in everyday life in India, and visiting cities such as Delhi and Agra, even for those of no faith, often turns out to be a rewardingly spiritual experience. Places of worship may throng with devotees, but they usually welcome visitors too, and the time you spend in these serenely sacred spots will linger long in the memory.

Hinduism

More than 80% of the population in these two cities is Hindu. Worship and ritual are paramount in the role of Hinduism. In Hindu homes you'll often find a dedicated worship area, where members of the family pray to the deities of their choice. Beyond the home, Hindus worship at temples. *Puja* is a focal point of worship and ranges from silent prayer to elaborate ceremonies. Devotees leave the temple with a handful of *prasad* (temple-blessed food) which is shared among others. Other forms of worship include *aarti* (the auspicious lighting of lamps or candles) and the playing of *bhajans* (devotional songs).

Islam

Islam is this region's largest minority religion, followed by around 15% of people. It was introduced to northern India by Muslim conquerors, and reached its zenith during the Mughal Empire (1526–1761), which reigned at various times from Delhi, Agra and briefly from Fatehpur Sikri. Many of the cities' most famous monuments, including the Taj Mahal, the Red Fort, Agra Fort and Jama Masjid date from this period, and Delhi's Jama Masjid remains one of India's largest active mosques.

Best Temples

Gurdwara Bangla Sahib
Delhi's largest and most atmospheric gurdwara (Sikh temple). (pictured above; p64)

Akshardham Temple
Delhi's largest Hindu temple is decorated in

SAIKO3P/SHUTTERSTOCK ©

stunningly intricate stone carvings. (p92)

Digambara Jain Temple Red sandstone centre of worship for the Jain religion, built in 1658. (p44)

Best Mosques

Jama Masjid, Delhi Delhi's principal mosque overlooks the heart of Old Delhi. (p38)

Fatehpuri Masjid This 17th-century Old Delhi mosque is a haven of tranquillity after the frantic streets outside. (p45)

Jama Masjid, Fatehpur Sikri This beautiful, immense mosque was completed in 1571 and is entered through the spectacular 54m-high Buland Darwaza (Victory Gate). (p138)

Jama Masjid, Agra Built in the Kinari Bazaar by Shah Jahan's daughter in 1648, this fine mosque was once connected to Agra Fort and features striking zigzag marble patterning on its domes. (p130)

Best Spiritual Hubs

Gurdwara Bangla Sahib Delhi's principal gurdwara is always busy with devotees, and hugely welcoming towards visitors. (pictured above; p64)

Hazrat Nizam-ud-din Dargah Intensely holy Muslim shrine always crammed with followers, but Thursday evening *qawwali* (Islamic devotional singing) is particularly atmospheric. (p80)

Majnu-ka-Tilla Delhi's traffic-free Tibetan enclave offers a different take on spirituality with red-robed Buddhist monks wandering the alleys, and the scent of yak-butter in the air. (p50)

History

TRAVELVIEW/SHUTTERSTOCK ©

Best Mughal Monuments

Taj Mahal Emperor Shah Jahan's exquisite marble masterpiece. (p122)

Fatehpur Sikri Astonishing abandoned city, just outside Agra. (p136)

Red Fort The formidable Delhi home of Mughal emperors for nearly 200 years. (p34)

Agra Fort Emperor Akbar's riverside fortress. (p126)

Humayun's Tomb The most impressive of Delhi's numerous Mughal tombs. (p78)

Jama Masjid Delhi's largest and most important mosque. (p38)

Best Ruins

Qutab Minar Complex Astonishing Afghan-style victory tower and minaret, erected in 1193. (p108)

Mehrauli Archaeological Park Forested park containing more than 400 historical monuments from across the eras. (p110)

Hauz Khas Funky cafes and clothing boutiques beside the remains of a 14th-century madrasa (Islamic college) overlooking an ancient water tank. (p99)

Agrasen ki Baoli Atmospheric 14th-century stepwell now finding itself in the middle of a city. (p65)

Fatehpur Sikri The long-abandoned, short-lived capital of Emperor Akbar. (p136)

Best Colonial-Era History

Rajpath Vast avenue linking India Gate to the offices of the Indian government. (p58)

India Gate Iconic stone war-memorial arch. (p65)

Connaught Place Circular, colonnaded, shopping district named after George V's uncle, the Duke of Connaught. (pictured above; p64)

Best Forts

Agra Fort Commanding red-sandstone fortress, looking out towards the Taj. (p126)

Red Fort Delhi's signature tourist attraction. (p34)

Purana Qila The 'Old Fort' is smaller in scale than the Red Fort, but can be explored more freely. (p76)

Tughlaqabad This magnificent 14th-century ruined fort was Delhi's third incarnation. (p114)

Best Mausoleums

Taj Mahal The ultimate expression of love. (p122)

Humayun's Tomb An arresting precursor to the Taj Mahal. (p78)

Hazrat Nizam-ud-din Dargah Marble shrine of Muslim Sufi saint Nizam-ud-din Auliya, hidden in a tangle of bazaars and thronging with devotees. (p80)

MATYAS REHAK/SHUTTERSTOCK ©

Best Delhi Tours

Street Connections Fascinating walk through Old Delhi, guided by former street children. (p47)

DelhiByCycle The original, and best cycle tours of the city. (p47)

Best Agra Tours

Agra by Bike Bike tours of the city and surrounding countryside, most of which end with a boat trip on the Yamuna River behind the Taj. (p131)

Agra Walks Walking/ cycle-rickshaw combo tour showing you sides of the city most tourists don't see. (p130)

Amin Tours All-inclusive private Agra day trips from Delhi by car. (p130)

UP Tourism Whistle-stop bus tours of Agra run by the state tourism office. (p131)

Best Wellness

Tushita Mahayana Meditation Centre Twice-weekly guided Buddhist meditation sessions in a temple-like meditation hall. (p101)

Sivananda Yoga There's a free introductory drop-in class on Sundays at this excellent yoga ashram. (p100)

Kerala Ayurveda Good-value massage treatments. (p101)

Amatrra Spa Where the A-List come to be pampered. (p85)

Best Green Spaces

Lodi Garden Lush, tree-shaded park, dotted with 15th-century tombs; a favourite for local joggers. (p83)

Purana Qila The landscaped grounds inside Delhi's 'Old Fort' are great for picnics. (p76)

Sunder Nursery Fruit trees, butterflies and Mughal monuments. (p83)

Mehrauli Archaeological Park Monkey-filled forested park on the city's outskirts containing more than 400 ruined monuments. (pictured above; p110)

Mehtab Bagh Historic riverside park in Agra, with sublime views of the Taj. (p130)

Museums

Delhi's museums range from grand, all-encompassing affairs, to quirky numbers that will pique specialist interests. With the exception of the National Museum and National Gallery of Modern Art, most are either free to enter or very cheap. Most are closed on Mondays. Agra has few museums, though there is a small one within the grounds of the Taj.

AZHAR_KHAN/SHUTTERSTOCK ©

Best History Museums

National Museum Delhi's best. (p64)

National Gandhi Museum Dedicated to the life, and tragic death, of the great mahatma. (p66)

Taj Museum Small but excellent museum within the Taj grounds, housing Mughal miniature paintings, old coins and the like. (p123)

Best Cultural Museums

Crafts Museum A largely outdoor museum showcasing traditional crafts from different regions of India. (p66)

Sanskriti Museums This is also largely outdoors; devoted to traditional Indian art. (p113)

Gandhi Darshan Landscaped gardens with various exhibition rooms, and a pavilion devoted to Gandhi photos. (p66)

Tibet House Showing valuable Tibetan items. (p85)

Best Quirky Museums

Sulabh International Museum of Toilets Offbeat museum with a social message. (p118)

Shankar's International Dolls Museum More than 7000 dolls from 85 different countries. (p67)

National Rail Museum The ultimate day out for train buffs. (pictured above; p84)

Best Art Museums

National Gallery of Modern Art Delhi's flagship art gallery. (p66)

Kiran Nadar Museum of Art Stylish contemporary art museum located in Saket. (p119)

For Kids

There's lots that children will enjoy in Delhi and Agra, though both cities are sensory onslaughts no matter how old you are, so taking it easy is key. Staying in quiet suburbs, or in homestay-type accommodation, will make for a less hectic experience. South Indian food is less spicy than North India's Mughlai cuisine.

RAVINDERKANYAL/SHUTTERSTOCK ©

The Experience

India isn't an obvious family destination, but kids, just like adults, will be fascinated by the intensity of the experience; just sharing pavements with cows and monkeys will delight most children, and the colours, sounds and unusual sights will hold the attention of even the most reluctant teenage traveller. And if all else fails, hop on a cycle-rickshaw; kids love them.

Need to Know

Nappies are widely available, but baby-change facilities are almost non-existent. There's a reason locals don't use pushchairs: lack of pavements in many places, the traffic and the crowds generally make them more of a hindrance than a help; you'll be much better off bringing a sling or a baby ruck-sack for toddlers.

Best Family-Friendly Sights & Activities

National Rail Museum Hugely enjoyable museum with steam locos, a miniature railway and two simulators. (p84)

Lodi Garden Perfect family picnic territory. (p83)

Purana Qila Rambling ruins for the young explorer. (pictured above; p76)

DelhiByCycle Professionally run cycle tours of Delhi – great fun for families. (p47)

Street Connections Walking tours of Old Delhi run by former street children. (p47)

Four Perfect Days

Day 1

DAVE STAMBOULIS/ALAMY STOCK PHOTO ©

Head to Delhi's **Red Fort** (p34) before the crowds arrive, and spend the morning exploring its vast grounds.

For lunch, tuck into mouthwatering mutton and flatbreads at Old Delhi's famous Muslim eatery **Karim's** (p46), close to **Jama Masjid** (p38), Delhi's largest mosque. From the mosque, you can dive into the maze of **old-city bazaars** (p52) – see if you can find your way to the sneeze-inducing **Spice Market** (pictured above; p53)!

Come evening, dine in style at **Lakhori** (p48), a regal-like restaurant inside the beautifully restored courtyard hotel, Haveli Dharampura, then hop in a cab to Connaught Place where you can drink under a banyan tree and listen to live music in the courtyard bar, **Unplugged** (p70).

Day 2

SAMOP/SHUTTERSTOCK ©

Take the Delhi metro south to spend the morning at the sublime **Qutab Minar** (pictured above; p108), but don't miss exploring the tree-shaded ruins of nearby **Mehrauli Archaeological Park** (p110).

Lunch at the refined Mediterranean courtyard restaurant **Olive** (p117) before travelling a couple of stops north on the metro to **Hauz Khas** (p99), a small arts enclave with clothing boutiques, bars, coffee shops and the ruins of Feroz Shah's 14th-century **madrasa** (p99) and **tomb** (p99), all overlooking a forest-fringed lake.

Stay in Hauz Khas for an evening meal at the temple-like south-Indian restaurant **Naivedyam** (p101), then shuffle your way around the corner to **Hauz Khas Social** (p103), a buzzing hotspot.

Day 3

Spend the morning in Delhi's peaceful, tree-shaded **Lodi Garden** (pictured above; p83), before taking an autorickshaw to the magnificent **Humayun's Tomb** (p78).

Cross the main road to the Hazrat Nizam-ud-din complex for grilled skewers at the **Kebab Stands** (p87) before weaving your way through the covered alleyways to the incredible **Hazrat Nizam-ud-din Dargah** (p80), the shrine of Muslim Sufi saint Nizam-ud-din Auliya, and one of the most magically spiritual corners of Delhi.

Hop in a cab to Paharganj, Delhi's backpacker central, for a delicious, no-frills dinner at **Tadka** (p49) and a stroll along busy **Main Bazaar** (p54) before taking an evening train to Agra for tomorrow's date with the Taj Mahal.

Day 4

Make an early start so you can soak up all the magic of the **Taj Mahal** (pictured above; p122) before the crowds arrive – don't miss seeing the **Taj Museum** (p123) before you leave.

For lunch head to *chaat galli* (snack alley) in Sadar Bazaar – try **Agra Chat House** (p132) for traditional snacks, or else the excellent **Mama Chicken** (p131). Then take an auto to **Mehtab Bagh** (p130), a charming Mughal park with views of the Taj from the other side of the Yamuna River.

Visit the immense **Agra Fort** (p126) on your way back before enjoying a simple evening meal with magical views of the Taj from the rooftop restaurant at **Saniya Palace Hotel** (p133).

Need to Know

For detailed information, see Survival Guide p141

Currency
Indian rupees (₹)

Languages Spoken
Hindi, Urdu, English

Visas
Most nationals can stay for up to 60 days with a hassle-free, double-entry, e-Visa (www.indianvisaonline.gov.in/evisa). Longer stays (up to six months) require a standard tourist visa.

Money
ATMs are everywhere. Cards are accepted at many hotels, shops and restaurants.

Mobile Phones
You can use your unlocked mobile phone on roaming, but it's much cheaper to buy a local SIM card. You'll need your passport to register a local SIM, and your accommodation details.

Time
India Standard Time; IST (UTC/GMT plus 5½ hours)

Daily Budget

Budget: Less than ₹2500
Budget hotel/dorm room: ₹400–800
Thali meals: ₹100–200
Entry to big sights: ₹300–600
Ticket on Delhi Metro: ₹10–60

Midrange: ₹2500–10,000
Double room in a midrange hotel: ₹2000–5000
Meals in a midrange restaurant: ₹500–1000
Admission to sights: ₹300–600
Short taxi trip: ₹100–250

Top end: More than ₹10,000
Luxury hotel room: from ₹10,000
Meal in a top-end restaurant: from ₹2000
Hiring a car and driver for a day tour: from ₹2000
Massage at a Delhi spa: from ₹4000

Advance Planning

Three months before Arrange volunteer placements or other long-term courses.

One month before Book accommodation if you plan to stay in unusual boutique lodgings.

One week before Download apps, such as Ola Cabs, that you might use in India. Book at least your first night's accommodation, and arrange an airport pick-up if arriving at night.

Arriving in Delhi & Agra

Most travellers will arrive in Delhi by air, and in Agra by train.

✈ Indira Gandhi International Airport

Metro The Airport Express line (5.15am to 11.40pm, every 10 minutes) runs from Terminal 3 to New Delhi train station (30 minutes).

Bus Air-conditioned buses run from outside Terminal 3 to Kashmere Gate ISBT (Delhi's main bus station) every 10 minutes.

Taxi In front of the arrivals buildings are counters offering fixed-price taxi services.

🚐 Agra Cantonment (Cantt) train station

Early-morning express trains are well set up for day trippers from Delhi, but trains run to/from Delhi all day, taking two to 3½ hours.

For fixed-price fares into town, there are prepaid taxi and autorickshaw booths outside the station.

Getting Around

Delhi has an extensive metro system. Agra doesn't, so you'll be mostly using autorickshaws.

Ⓜ Metro

Delhi's metro system is cheap, easy to use, and expanding, and has pretty much ended the need to use the city's hectic local buses.

🚗 Autorickshaw

Autorickshaws (pictured below) are everywhere, especially in Delhi. E-rickshaws are an environmentally friendly electric alternative.

🚗 Cycle rickshaw

Great fun, cheaper than autorickshaws. Tip generously.

🚗 Taxi

Taxi apps (Uber) are beginning to supersede ordinary taxis.

Delhi & Agra Neighbourhoods

New Delhi (p57)
Great for shopping, eating and drinking, and sprinkled with architectural reminders of the British Raj.

Sunder Nagar, Nizamuddin & Lodi Colony (p75)
A sweeping neighbourhood with some of the city's best parks and most alluring historical sites. Great markets, too.

Indira Gandhi
International
Airport

South Delhi (p95)
Affluent, leafy, city-centre escape with trendy markets, historic parks and plenty of good restaurants.

Greater Delhi & Gurgaon (Gurugram) (p107)
Vast neighbourhood including some standout archaeological ruins as well as the malls, food courts and sky-trains of modern Gurgaon.

Red Fort

Jama
Masjid

Old Delhi (p33)
A mesmerising medley of
mosques, markets, temples,
bells, bazaars, incense,
rickshaws, cows, hawkers,
monkeys, alleyways, street
food and honking horns.

Rajpath

Akshardham
Temple

Purana Qila

Hazrat
Nizam-ud-
din Dargah

Humayun's
Tomb

Qutab Minar
Complex

Mehrauli
Archaeological
Park

Agra (p121)
The Taj Mahal, Agra Fort
and Fatehpur Sikri make
up Agra's golden trio of
must-see Unesco-listed
sights.

Agra (300km) ↓

Explore
Delhi & Agra

Colourful Old Delhi shop SAIKO3P/SHUTTERSTOCK ©

Explore ⊕
Old Delhi (Shahjahanabad)

The beating heart of Delhi, this incredible neighbour-hood will knock you sideways with the power of its sights, sounds and smells, and with the unrelenting chaos of its magical street bazaars. But if you can survive that first hit, you'll soon realise you've just landed in one of the world's truly special places. Prepare to be amazed.

The Short List

o **Red Fort (p34)** *Crossing the threshold of the immense fortress that was home to Mughal emperors for more than 200 years.*

o **Jama Masjid (p38)** *Taking a spiritual timeout in the calming atmosphere inside Delhi's largest mosque.*

o **Chandni Chowk (p44)** *Getting lost in the myriad street-bazaars that branch off from this fun, but frantic main thoroughfare.*

o **Spice Market (p53)** *Trying in vain to hold back the sneezes inside India's largest spice market, before climbing the roof for sweeping city views.*

o **Main Bazaar (p54)** *Diving into the chaotic heart of Paharganj; Delhi's backpacker hub.*

Getting There & Around

Ⓜ Handy stations include Jama Masjid, Lal Qila, Chawri Bazaar and, for Paharganj, Ramakrishna Ashram Marg.

🚶 Once here it's often quickest to travel around on foot.

Rickshaws Cycle rickshaws are another option; handy for slightly longer distances.

Neighbourhood Map on p42

Chandni Chowk (p44) AMIT KG/SHUTTERSTOCK ©

Top Sight
Red Fort

Founded by Emperor Shah Jahan and surrounded by a magnificent 18m-high wall, this immense fort took 10 years to construct (1638–48) and went on to become home to Mughal emperors for more than 200 years. Once a lavish abode of exquisite palaces, gardens and rose-scented waterways, it's now a shell of its former self, but still makes for an intriguing visit.

◎ MAP P42, G3

Indian/foreigner ₹50/600, with card payment ₹35/550, video ₹25, audio guide in Hindi/English or Korean ₹69/118

🕑 dawn-dusk Tue-Sun

Ⓜ Chandni Chowk

Making an Entrance

Lahore Gate is the main entrance to the fort, and takes its name from the fact that it faces the city of Lahore, in modern-day Pakistan. If one spot could be said to be the emotional and symbolic heart of modern India, it is this magnificent gateway. During the struggles for Independence, one of the nationalists' declarations was that they would see the Indian flag flying over the Red Fort. After Independence, many important political speeches were given by Nehru and Indira Gandhi to the crowds amassed on the grounds outside, and now on Independence Day each year the prime minister addresses the people from Lahore Gate. This is also where you, as a tourist, will enter the complex, and it is quite an entrance.

Paradise on Earth

Though today, as with all the buildings inside the fort, the **Diwan-i-Khas** (Hall of Private Audiences) is a pale shadow of its former self, this colonnaded hall was once so lavish that its walls were inscribed with the Persian couplet: 'If there is paradise on the earth, it is this, it is this, it is this'.

Built of white marble, this luxurious chamber sits at the end of the central pathway that leads across the complex from Lahore Gate, and was where the emperor would hold private meetings. Its latticed screens once overlooked the Yamuna River (now a ring road) and it was cooled by a channel of water known as the Stream of Paradise (Nahar-i-Bihisht). Its centrepiece was the legendary **Peacock Throne**; a gold-encrusted throne with figures of peacocks, inlaid with precious stones, standing behind it. Between them was the figure of a parrot, carved out of a single emerald. The throne was captured and taken as a war trophy in 1739 by the Persian emperor Nadir Shah, and has been lost ever

★ Top Tips

○ Rent an audio guide from the ticket office, rather than paying for the services of one of the many unofficial guides who prey on tourists by the main gate.

○ Bring plenty of water and snacks. The grounds are vast and quite exposed, and there's nowhere to buy supplies.

○ Come early to avoid the crowds. The fort opens at dawn, and is practically empty until 9am or 10am.

✕ Take a Break

There's nowhere to buy food inside, but Old Delhi's culinary delights are on your doorstep. On or just off Chandni Chowk, you'll find Jalebi Wala (p47), Natraj Dahi Balle Corner (p46) and PT Gaya Prasad Shiv Charan (p47) each serving different types of delectable Delhi street food.

since. The marble platform it once sat on does, though, remain inside.

In 1760, the Marathas also removed the silver ceiling from the hall. This is, nevertheless, still the most elegant building within the fort, and you can still see some of the beautiful inlaid floral designs on the lower parts of its marble columns.

Nearby is **Diwan-i-Am**, an arcade of sandstone columns that was the hall of public audience, where the emperor greeted guests and dignitaries from a throne on the raised marble platform, which is backed by fine pietra dura (inlaid stone) work that features Orpheus, incongruously, and is thought to be Florentine.

Pleasure Gardens

The grounds within the fort were once designed along the lines of a classic Mughal garden, a rectilinear layout with pools, fountains and canals amongst tree-shaded, flower-filled lawns and beds. These days much of the greenery has been lost, and the water channels and fountains are dry, but there is still some shade under the few remaining mature trees, which make nice spots to rest up with a drink and a snack.

What's in a Name?

The fort wasn't originally called Lal Qila (Red Fort). Shah Jahan named it Qila Mubarak (Blessed Fort), while the later Mughals called it Qila-e-Mullah (Exalted Fort). Back then all the buildings within the fort, though not the outer walls, were covered in white plaster, gilding and paintwork, and the white-marble sections were decorated with jewel-filled pietra dura inlay work. Only later, as the plaster and decoration began to wear off, or was plundered, did the fort's buildings reveal their red-sandstone foundations.

Latest Facelift

Controversially, in 2018 the Government leased out the job of maintaining the fort to a private firm, the Dalmia Bharat group, prompting accusations from conservationists that it had sold the country's heritage. Dalmia soon began wholesale renovations, including laying new red-sandstone pathways over some of the existing quartzite stone paths.

At the time of research, all the fort's museums were closed during renovations, and with the exception of the arcades at **Chatta Chowk** and **Diwan-i-Am**, none of the fort's buildings could be entered. It was unclear when the renovations would be finished, but the main structures are expected to reopen once the work is complete.

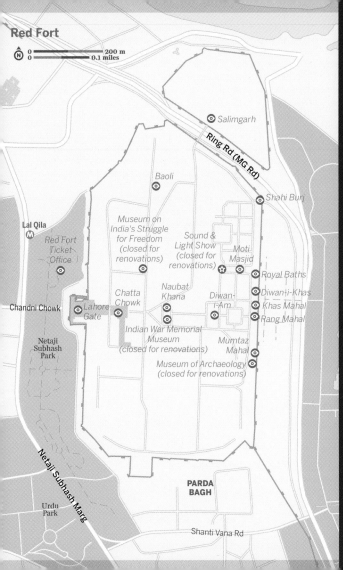

Red Fort

N 0 ——————— 200 m
   0 ——————— 0.1 miles

Salimgarh

Ring Rd (MG Rd)

Baoli

Shahi Burj

Lal Qila

Red Fort
Ticket
Office

Museum on
India's Struggle
for Freedom
(closed for
renovations)

Sound &
Light Show
(closed for
renovations)

Moti
Masjid

Royal Baths

Diwan-i-Khas

Chandni Chowk

Lahore
Gate

Chatta
Chowk

Naubat
Khana

Diwan-
i-Am

Khas Mahal

Rang Mahal

Netaji
Subhash
Park

Indian War Memorial
Museum
(closed for renovations)

Mumtaz
Mahal

Museum of Archaeology
(closed for renovations)

Netaji Subhash Marg

Urdu
Park

PARDA
BAGH

Shanti Vana Rd

Top Sight 📷
Jama Masjid

A beautiful pocket of calm at the heart of Old Delhi's mayhem, the capital's largest mosque is built on a 10m elevation, towering above the surrounding hubbub, and can hold a mind-blowing 25,000 people.

◉ **MAP P42, F4**

Friday Mosque

camera & video each ₹300, tower ₹100

🕐 non-Muslims 8am-1hr before sunset, minaret 9am-5.30pm

Ⓜ Jama Masjid

Architecture

The marble and red-sandstone structure was Shah Jahan's final architectural triumph, built between 1644 and 1658. The four corner **watchtowers** were used for security. There are also two **minarets** standing 40m high, one of which can be climbed for incredible views of the surrounding area; from the top, the discerning will be able to notice how architect Edwin Lutyens incorporated the mosque into his design of New Delhi – the Jama Masjid, Connaught Place and Sansad Bhavan (Parliament House) are in a direct line.

Notable features inside include the huge chandelier hung inside the main chamber.

Visiting the Mosque

There are numerous entrance gates, but only Gate 1 (south side), Gate 2 (east) and Gate 3 (north) allow access to the mosque for visitors.

The security guards aren't the friendliest people in Delhi – especially if you don't bring a camera and dispute why you should have to pay the ₹300 'photography fee' – but once inside, you'll find a warm welcome from locals, and a pleasant, calming atmosphere; bring a book and soak it up. Once inside, you can buy a separate ₹100 ticket to climb the 121 steps up the narrow southern minaret (notices say that unaccompanied women are not permitted).

Note, that the mosque closes to non-Muslims during main prayer times (usually for an hour around noon and around 4pm, though times vary). Also, legs and arms must be covered up. To avoid having to 'borrow' (often for a small fee) one of the body-length robes from security staff, wear full-length trousers, and bring a shawl to cover your shoulders and arms.

★ Top Tips

o If you don't want to pay the ₹300 'photography fee' levied at foreigners, leave behind your camera, phone, and any device that might be deemed able to take photographs.

o Shoes cannot be worn inside, but do as locals do and carry yours inside with you rather than paying to leave them at the entrance. That way you'll be free to exit the mosque from other gates.

✕ Take a Break

You can brings snacks and water inside, but for proper food you'll need to exit the mosque. Old Delhi's most famous restaurant, Karim's (p46), is a short walk from Gate 1. For a coffee with a view over the mosque, head to the rooftop cafe on top of Hotel Aiwan-e-Shahi (p52), just outside Gate 3.

Old Delhi (Shahjahanabad) Jama Masjid

Walking Tour 🥾

Bazaars of Old Delhi

Old Delhi's bazaars are a bamboozling, sensual whirlwind, combining incense, spices, rickshaw fumes, brilliant colours, and hole-in-the-wall shops packed with goods that shimmer and glitter. This is less retail therapy, more heightened reality. The best time to visit is mid-morning or later in the day, when the streets are less busy.

Walk Facts

Start Red Fort; Ⓜ Lal Qila

End Spice Market; Ⓜ Chandni Chowk

Length 3.5km; three to four hours

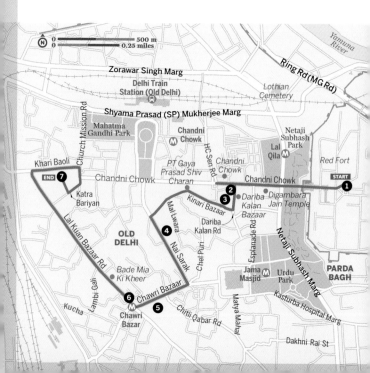

❶ Red Fort

Start with your back to the iconic Red Fort (p34) and walk directly away from it, along the left-hand side of busy Chandni Chowk (p44). You'll soon pass the red-sandstone Digambara Jain Temple (p44) on your left as you shuffle your way along this startlingly hectic thoroughfare, before reaching Old Delhi's famous and easy-to-spot snack stall, Jalebi Wala.

❷ Jalebi Wala

Time to tuck in to some of Delhi's famous street-food (p47); a supersticky, syrup-sweet coil of deep-fried *jalebi*. Fingers licked clean and energy levels boosted, you're ready to dive into the narrow alleys for some proper street-bazaar action.

❸ Kinari Bazaar

Walk down the alley beside Jalebi Wala, called Dariba Kalan Bazaar (p53), which shines with silver jewellery, ornaments and coins, then after 150m turn right up colourful Kinari Bazaar (p52), a fabulously photogenic street market famous for *zardozi* (gold embroidery), temple trim and wedding turbans.

❹ Nai Sarak

After 350m, just before you reach PT Gaya Prasad Shiv Charan (p47), which serves delicious stuffed *paratha* (flaky flatbread), turn left and follow the lane to the crossroads (300m). Here turn left onto Nai Sarak (p53), another colourful bazaar lined with stalls selling saris and shawls, until you reach the main road, called Chawri Bazaar.

❺ Chawri Bazaar

This wider **market street** (🕙10am-7pm; Ⓜ Chawri Bazar) is known for its wrapping paper and wedding cards. Turn right onto it, then right again when you reach the roundabout above Chawri Bazaar metro station.

❻ Lal Kuan Main Bazaar

You're now walking along gritty, non-touristy **Lal Kuan Main Bazaar** (🕙10am-8pm; Ⓜ Jama Masjid), which sells cooking pots and other steel containers, as well as pretty paper kites. Not far along, on your right, at No 2867, you'll find the wonderful Bade Mia Ki Kheer (p47), which has been serving cardamon-scented *kheer* (rice pudding) since 1880.

❼ Spice Market

Continue to the end of the road, turn right, then, after about 200m, duck into the Spice Market (p53) on your right. This is the largest spice market in India, and you'll be sneezing as soon as you walk in. Complete a circuit around the inner courtyard, then take the steps up to the rooftop for panoramic city views.

Old Delhi (Shahjahanabad)

A **B** **C** **D**

1

Pul Bangash

Tis Hazari

Lala Hardev Sahai Marg

Gokhale Marg

Nicholson Rd

Tilak Gali

Zorawar Singh Marg

For reviews see
- ◉ Top Sights p34
- ◎ Sights p44
- ✗ Eating p46
- 🍷 Drinking p51
- ★ Entertainment p52
- 🔒 Shopping p52

2

Church Mission Rd

Mahatma Gandhi Park

Sadar Bazaar Train Station

Fatehpuri Town Masjid Hall

Khari Baoli **34**

Chandni Chowk

3

SADAR BAZAAR

Dr Ram Manohar Lohia Marg

Idgah Rd

Qutb Rd

Lal Kuan Bazaar Rd

4

RAM NAGAR

Lambi Gali

✗**12**

Chawri Bazar

Kuremal Mohan Lal

Ajmeri Gate

5

21 **14**
✗ ✗

26

25 Arakashan Rd

Desh Bandhu Gupta Rd

New Delhi

New Delhi Train Station

Chitragupta Rd

Rajguru Rd

Sang Trashan Rd

State Entry Rd

Bhavbuti Rd

Radial Rd 5

6

15✗

37🔒

RK Ashram Marg

20
✗

27🔒

16🔒

40 **41**
🔒 🔒

23
✗

22 **39**
✗ 🔒

17 **36**
✗ 🔒

Main Bazaar

PAHARGANJ

Basant Rd

Chelmsford Rd

Panchkuian Marg

7

Ramakrishna Mission

A **B** **C** **D**

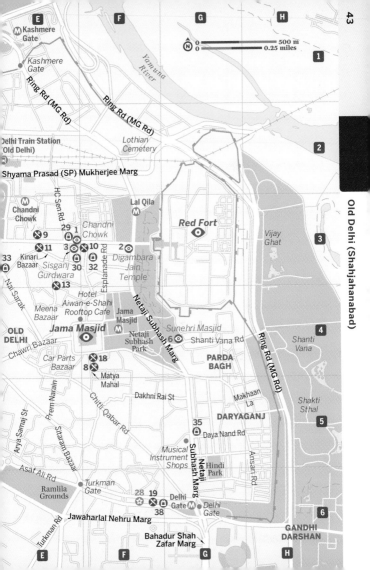

Sights

Chandni Chowk   AREA

1 ⊙ MAP P42, E3

Old Delhi's main drag is lined by
Jain, Hindu and Sikh temples,
plus a church, with the Fatehpuri
Masjid at one end. Tree-lined and
elegant in Mughal times, the thoroughfare is now mind-bendingly
chaotic, with tiny little ancient
bazaars tentacling off it. In the
Mughal era, Chandni Chowk centred on a pool that reflected the
moon, hence the name, 'moon-
light place'. The main street is
almost impossible to cross, full as
it is of cars, hawkers, motorcycles,
rickshaws and porters. (Ⓜ Chandni
Chowk)

Digambara Jain Temple   JAIN TEMPLE

2 ⊙ MAP P42, F3

Opposite the Red Fort is the red
sandstone Digambara Jain Temple,
built in 1658. Interestingly, it
houses a **bird hospital** (donations
appreciated; ⊙10am-5pm) established in 1956 to further the Jain
principle of preserving all life, treat-
ing 30,000 birds a year. Remove
shoes and leather items before entering the temple. (Chandni Chowk;
⊙6am-noon & 6-9pm; Ⓜ Lal Qila)

Sisganj Gurdwara   SIKH TEMPLE

3 ⊙ MAP P42, E3

The icing-sugar-white 18th-century
Sisganj Gurdwara marks the mar-
trydom site of the ninth Sikh guru,

The Gateways of Old Delhi

The 17th-century walled city of Shahjahanabad, now referred to as
Old Delhi, was once accessed through 14 immense gateways. Sadly,
the walls have largely been demolished, but some of the gateways still
remain, albeit now largely free-standing and somewhat incongruous.

Delhi Gate (Map p42, G6; Netaji Subhash Marg; Ⓜ Jama Masjid) Traffic
swirls around this historic city gate, built in 1638 as one of the main
entrances to the walled city.

Kashmere Gate (Map p42, E1; cnr Lothian & Nicholson Rds; Ⓜ Kashmere
Gate) This northernmost gate (leading to Kashmir) was the largest of
all the entrances to the walled city. It was only built in the 19th century,
and was damaged during the 1857 First War of Independence.

Ajmeri Gate (Map p42, D5; Ajmeri Gate Rd; Ⓜ New Delhi, Chawri Bazaar)
Over 300 years old, this lies opposite Ghazi-ud-Din's Tomb and
Mosque, built by a nobleman at the time of Aurangzeb.

Turkman Gate (Map p42, E6; Asaf Ali Rd; Ⓜ New Delhi) Named after Sufi
saint Hazrat Shah Turkman Bayabani, whose tomb lies to the east.

PAOLO QUERCI/SHUTTERSTOCK ©

Digambara Jain Temple

Tegh Bahadur, executed by Aurang-zeb in 1675 for resisting conversion to Islam. A banyan tree marks the spot where he was killed. (Chandni Chowk; M Chandni Chowk)

Fatehpuri Masjid   MOSQUE

4 ⦿ MAP P42, D3

Built by Fatehpuri Begum, one of Shah Jahan's wives, this 17th-century mosque is a haven of tranquillity after the frantic streets outside. The central pool was taken from a noble house, hence the elaborate shape. After the First War of Independence, the mosque was sold to a Hindu nobleman by the British for ₹19,000 and returned to Muslim worship in exchange for four villages 20 years later. (Chandni Chowk; ⏰5am-9.30pm; M Chandni Chowk)

Town Hall   HISTORIC BUILDING

5 ⦿ MAP P42, D3

Built in 1864, Delhi's Town Hall originally housed a library, the European Club and the Lawrence Institute. There was once a statue of Queen Victoria in the front gar-den, but after Independence this was replaced with that of Swami Shraddhanand, founder of the Arya Samaj Hindu religious movement. (Chandni Chowk; M Chandni Chowk)

Sunehri Masjid   MOSQUE

6 ⦿ MAP P42, G4

Built in 1721, this mosque has gild-ed domes, hence its name. In 1739, the Persian invader Nadir Shah stood on the roof and watched his soldiers massacre thousands of Delhi's inhabitants. The mosque is immediately south of the Red Fort; follow the moat. (Golden Mosque; ⊙dawn-dusk; Ⓜ Chandni Chowk)

Ramakrishna Mission

HINDU TEMPLE

7 ◉ MAP P42, B6

Amid the chaos of Paharganj, the temple that gives the metro station here its name is a wonderfully calming escape, with a landscaped garden leading to a simple meditation hall. The morning and evening *aarti* (auspicious lighting of lamps or candles), at 5am and sunset, are atmospheric times to visit. At other times, people simply meditate in peace. (Ramakrishna Ashram; www.rkm delhi.org; Ramakrishna Marg; ⊙5am-noon & 4-9pm Apr-Sep, 3.30-8.30pm Oct-Mar; Ⓜ Ramakrishna Ashram Marg)

Eating

Karim's

MUGHLAI $$

8 ✕ MAP P42, F4

Down a narrow alley off a lane leading south from Jama Masjid,

Karim's has been delighting carnivores since 1913. Expect meaty Mughlai treats such as mutton *burrah* (marinated chops), delicious mutton Mughlai, and the breakfast mutton-and-bread combo *nahari*. There are numerous branches, including at Nizamuddin West (p86), but this no-frills, multiroomed courtyard location is the oldest and best. (Gali Kababyan; mains ₹120-400; ⊙9am-12.30am; Ⓜ Jama Masjid)

Natraj Dahi Balle Corner

STREET FOOD $

9 ✕ MAP P42, E3

This tiny place on the corner of a narrow lane is famous for its *dahi bhalle* (fried lentil balls served with yoghurt) and deliciously crispy *aloo tikki* (spiced potato patties), each of which costs ₹50. You'll have to elbow your way to the front of the queue to get your share, but it's worth the effort. (1396 Chandni Chowk; plates ₹50; ⊙10.30am-11pm; Ⓜ Chandni Chowk)

In the Footsteps of George V

Delhi's **Coronation Durbar Site** (Shanti Swaroop Tyagi Marg; Ⓜ Model Town) is a historical oddity worth seeking out if you like exploring forgotten corners. Around 10km north of Old Delhi, a lone obelisk marks the site where King George V was declared emperor of India in 1911, and where the great durbars (fairs) were held to honour India's British overlords in 1877 and 1903. A few marble busts of British officials and a mammoth statue of George V decorate the neighbouring park. Take an autorickshaw from Model Town metro station (3km).

Walking & Cycling Old Delhi

Offering two-hour 'street walks' around Paharganj, guided by former street kids, **Salaam Baalak Trust** (SBT; ☎ 011-23586416; www.salaam baalaktrust.com; suggested donation ₹400; ☺10am-noon) is a 30-year-old charity founded by the mother of film director Mira Nair, following her 1988 hit film about the life of street children, *Salaam Bombay!* The guides tell you their own, often-shocking, stories and take you to a couple of the trust's 'contact points' near New Delhi train station. **Street Connections** (www.streetconnections.co.uk; 3hr walk ₹750; ☺9am-noon Mon-Sat) also explores the hidden corners of Old Delhi, starting at Jama Masjid and visiting small temples and crumbling *haveli* mansions before an e-rickshaw ride takes you to the sneeze-inducing spice market then to one of SBT's shelter homes.

For something a bit different, cycling company **DelhiByCycle** (☎ 9811723720; www.delhibycycle.com; per person ₹1850; ☺6.30-10am) is the original and the best, and a thrilling way to explore Delhi. Tours focus on specific neighbourhoods and start early to miss the worst of the traffic. The price includes chai and breakfast. Helmets and child seats available.

Jalebi Wala

SWEETS **$**

10 ✘ MAP P42, F3

Century-old Jalebi Wala does Delhi's – if not India's – finest *jalebis* (deep-fried, syrupy dough), so eat up and worry about the calories tomorrow. It's ₹50 per 100g-serving (roughly one piece). It also does a mean samosa. (Dariba Corner, Chandni Chowk; jalebis ₹50, samosas ₹25; ☺8am-10pm; Ⓜ Lal Qila)

PT Gaya Prasad Shiv Charan

STREET FOOD **$**

11 ✘ MAP P42, E3

This winding lane off Chandni Chowk has been dishing up its namesake *paratha* fresh off the *tawa* (hotplate) for generations, originally serving pilgrims at the time of the Mughals. Walk down it from Chandni Chowk, take two turns and you'll find this, the most popular *paratha* joint of many. Stuffings include green chilli, almond, banana and more. (34 Gali Paranthe Wali; parathas ₹60-70; ☺7am-10pm; Ⓜ Jama Masjid)

Bade Mia Ki Kheer

STREET FOOD **$**

12 ✘ MAP P42, D4

Established in 1880 and still run by the Siddique family, this friendly place makes nothing but super-delicious, creamy, cardamon-scented *kheer* (rice pudding), usually served cold but if you're

Ice Cream Masters ¶⚪⟍

Traditional Indian ice cream, or *kulfi*, is similar to the type of ice cream eaten in the West, both in appearance and taste. However it is denser and creamier, and unlike ice cream, *kulfi* is not whipped, resulting in a more solid frozen dessert. You'll find *kulfi* being sold all over Old Delhi, but few places are as intriguing as **Kuremal Mohan Lal** (Kuremal kulfi-walla; Map p42, D5; Kucha Pati Ram, off Sitaram Bazaar; kulfi ₹60; ⊗noon-11pm; ⓂChawri Bazaar).

The Kuremal family have been making *kulfi* since 1906, and serve up delicious options including pomegranate and rose from their small shop in this alluring part of Old Delhi. Lolly-sized versions cost ₹60. Giant iced fruit balls are ₹200. But beware pretenders with similarly named *kulfi* shops; the original is at shop No 526.

lucky and it has just made a batch, served hot. (Old Kheer Shop; shop 2867, Lal Kuan Bazaar; kheer ₹30; ⊗11am-late; ⓂChawri Bazaar)

Lakhori INDIAN $$$

13 ⊗ MAP P42, E3

This beautifully restored *haveli* is a labour of love by politician Vijay Goel, and it's good to see one of Old Delhi's grand *havelis* finally get some TLC. The restaurant is especially atmospheric in the evening, with tables in the courtyard and Mughlai and local recipes on the menu. Indian high tea (₹1100; 4pm to 6pm) is served daily on the rooftop. On weekends there is *kathak* dancing on the balcony. (☏011-23263000; www.haveli dharampura.com; Haveli Dharampura, 2293 Gali Guliyan; tasting menus veg/ nonveg ₹1800/2200; mains ₹500-900; ⊗noon-10.30pm; 🛜; ⓂJama Masjid)

Darbar INDIAN $

14 ⊗ MAP P42, B5

Considering its gritty Paharganj location and its street-food roots, the interior of this locals' favourite is surprisingly elegant. Street-food *chaat* (savoury snacks) are served by the entrance, while the main menu focuses on rich Mughlai curries, delicate South Indian delights such as dosa and *uttapam* (savoury rice pancake), and some outstanding thalis; the 10-piece Shahi thali (₹240) is a feast. (Multani Dhanda, Paharganj; snacks ₹30-100, dishes ₹125-270, thalis ₹210-260; ⊗8.30am-11.30pm; ⓂRamakrishna Ashram Marg)

Sita Ram Dewan Chand INDIAN $

15 ⊗ MAP P42, A6

A family-run hole-in-the-wall serving inexpensive portions of just one dish – *chole bhature* (spicy chickpeas, accompanied by delicious, freshly made, puffy, fried bread with a light paneer filling). It's a traditional breakfast in Delhi, but many people are partial to some at any time of day. There are no seats; instead diners stand at high tables to eat. Lassis cost ₹40. (2243 Chuna Mandi; half/full plate ₹35/60; ⊙8am-6pm; Ⓜ Ramakrishna Ashram Marg)

Tadka INDIAN $$

16 Ⓧ MAP P42, B6

Named for everyone's favourite dhal, Tadka's no-frills interior and relatively low prices belie its fabulously tasty menu, which includes delicious dhal (naturally), some rich, creamy paneer dishes and standout roti and naan bread. The *dum aloo* (potato skins stuffed with paneer in a tomato sauce) is divine. (4986 Ramdwara Rd; mains ₹180-210; ⊙9am-10.30pm; ⵣ; Ⓜ Ramakrishna Ashram Marg)

Exotic Rooftop Restaurant MULTICUISINE $$

17 Ⓧ MAP P42, B6

Currently the most popular of the numerous rooftop restaurants and cafes overlooking frenetic Tooti Chowk, Exotic is a small laid-back place with a breezy perch and a decent please-all backpacker menu (biryani, pizza, falafel, pancakes). There's no lift, so you'll have to climb up four flights of stairs, but there are cold beers (₹180) waiting for you at the top. (Tooti Chowk, Main Bazaar, Paharganj; mains ₹200-400; ⊙8am-11.30pm; Ⓜ Ramakrishna Ashram Marg)

Desserts for sale at Kuremal Mohan Lal

Delhi's Tibetan Quarter

Majnu-ka-Tilla (Tibetan Colony, Majnu-ka-Tilla; ⏱around 10am-8pm; Ⓜ Vidhan Sabha) is an enclave that has served as a base for Tibetan refugees since around 1960, and its network of traffic-free alleyways is a fascinating place to shop for Tibetan trinkets and Buddhist-themed souvenirs.

There's a small **Buddhist temple** at one end of the enclave, and plenty of Tibetans and maroon-robed Buddhist monks wandering the lanes, which are dotted with small shops, cafes and restaurants.

For souvenirs, **Akama** (Majnu-ka-Tilla; ⏱9.30am-8.30pm; Ⓜ Vidhan Sabha) is a good-value Tibetan boutique selling purses, prayer flags, felt toys, Himalayan handmade soaps, tea cups and other trinkets.

There are some lovely cafes too; **Ama** (H40 Tibetan Colony, Majnu-ka-Tilla; dishes ₹150-300, coffee from ₹85; ⏱7am-9.45pm; 📶; Ⓜ Vidhan Sabha) being the most popular.

For Tibetan food, you can get *momos* (Tibetan dumplings) and *thukpa* (Tibetan noodle soup) at the long-running, no-frills **Dolma House** (Block 10, Tibetan Colony, Majnu-ka-Tilla; dishes ₹100-200; ⏱8am-10pm; Ⓜ Vidhan Sabha), or the smarter, but still cheap, **Tee Dee** (32 Tibetan Colony, Majnu-ka-Tilla; dishes ₹100-200; ⏱9.30am-8.30pm; Ⓜ Vidhan Sabha).

The enclave is 2km from Vidhan Sabha metro station; turn right out of Gate 2, then right at the second set of traffic lights, and cross the busy main road at the end (there's a footbridge). It's ₹30 to ₹40 in an autorickshaw.

Al-Jawahar

MUGHLAI $$

18 🍴 MAP P42, F4

Although overshadowed by its famous neighbour, Karim's (p46), Al-Jawahar is also fantastic, serving up tasty Mughlai cuisine at Formica tables in an orderly dining room, and you can watch breads being freshly made at the front. Kebabs and mutton curries dominate the menu, but it also does good butter chicken and korma. (Matya Mahal; dishes ₹110-400; ⏱7am-midnight; Ⓜ Jama Masjid)

Chor Bizarre

KASHMIRI $$$

19 🍴 MAP P42, F6

Hotel Broadway's excellent, if quirky, restaurant has wood-panelling, traditional wooden furniture and fascinating bits of bric-a-brac, including a vintage car. More importantly it offers delicious and authentic Kashmiri cuisine, including *wazwan*, the traditional Kashmiri feast. (📞011-23273821; Hotel Broadway, 4/15 Asaf Ali Rd; mains ₹325-500; ⏱noon-3pm & 7.30-11pm; Ⓜ New Delhi)

Shim Tur
KOREAN $$

20 MAP P42, B6

The Korean food is fresh and authentic here; try the *bibimbap* (rice bowl with vegetables, egg and pickles; ₹270). But it takes determination to find this place: take the turning for the Hotel Rak International, opposite which is the grotty, unsigned Navrang Guesthouse. Follow the signs to its rooftop and you'll find the small, bamboo-lined, softly lit terrace. (3rd fl, Navrang Guesthouse, Tooti Gali; meals ₹200-500; 10.30am-11pm; M Ramakrishna Ashram Marg)

Bikaner Sweet Corner
SWEETS $

21 MAP P42, B5

This popular local sweet shop is the place in Paharganj to come for your evening treats; try the *kaju barfi* (cashew-milk sweet wrapped in silver leaf) or the *gajar halwa* (crumbly carrot dessert served with crushed nuts). Also sells dried fruit and nuts plus other savoury snacks. Sweets are sold by weight; 100g (₹50 to ₹125) gets you six or seven pieces. (Multani Dhanda, Paharganj; 7.30am-11pm; M Ramakrishna Ashram Marg)

Satguru Dhaba
INDIAN $

22 MAP P42, B6

Eat like a local rather than a tourist at this popular Paharganj *dhaba* (simple roadside eatery). It's no frills, for sure, but the food is tasty, as are the prices. From Main Bazaar, walk up Chandi Wali Gali, past Hotel Namaskar. Turn left at the end and it's on your left. English menu, but no English sign. (854 Mantola Mohalla, Paharganj; dishes ₹50-250, thalis ₹100; 8am-midnight; M Ramakrishna Ashram Marg)

Krishna Cafe
MULTICUISINE $

23 MAP P42, B6

There's a friendly welcome at this small, but popular, rooftop restaurant overlooking Main Bazaar's frenetic Tooti Chowk. The multicuisine menu includes all-day breakfasts, and the 'special tea' tastes remarkably similar to beer (nudge-nudge, wink-wink). (Chhe Tooti Chowk, Main Bazaar; dishes ₹100-250; 7.30am-10.30pm; M Ramakrishna Ashram Marg)

Drinking

PT Ved Prakash Lemon Wale
JUICE BAR

24 MAP P42, D3

Quenching Chandni Chowk's thirst for over a century now, this stalwart has a menu comprising just one item: homegrown fizzy lemonade that comes from a glass bottle sealed with a marble. Summer days find this hole-in-the-wall completely engulfed by loyal fans seeking much-needed relief from the Delhi heat. (011-23920931; 5466 Ghantaghar, Chandni Chowk; lemonade ₹10; 11.30am-10.30pm; M Chandni Chowk)

Coffee with a View

Welcoming non-guests to its small roof-terrace restaurant and coffee shop, **Hotel Aiwan-e-Shahi Rooftop Cafe** (Map p42, E4; ☏011-47155106; www.hotelaiwaneshahi.com; 1061 Dariba, near Jama Masjid Gate 3; Ⓜ Jama Masjid) has unrivalled views of Jama Masjid.

Cafe Brownie   CAFE

25 Ⓑ MAP P42, B5

Cute little cafe for an email catch-up, espresso in one hand, brownie or muffin in the other. (41 Arakashan Rd; coffee from ₹70; ◷7.30am-11pm; 📶; Ⓜ New Delhi)

Voyage Cafe   CAFE

26 Ⓑ MAP P42, B5

Cakes, shakes and very affordable Lavazza coffee, plus floor-to-ceiling windows for that full-on street-view experience. (8647 Arakashan Rd; coffee from ₹50; ◷24hr; 📶; Ⓜ New Delhi)

Sam's Bar   BAR

27 Ⓑ MAP P42, B6

If you can nab one of the two tables by the big window overlooking Main Bazaar this is a fine place to chill with a couple of beers (from ₹115). Sam's Bar is more laid-back than most Paharganj bars, with a mixed crowd of men and women, locals and foreigners. There's a full food menu as well as drinks. (Main Bazaar; ◷1pm-12.30am; Ⓜ Ramakrishna Ashram Marg)

Entertainment

Delite Cinema   CINEMA

28 ✪ MAP P42, F6

Founded in 1954 as the tallest building in Delhi, the Delite was renovated in 2006 and it's no ordinary cinema, with a painted dome and Czech chandeliers. It's a great place to see a masala picture (full-throttle Bollywood, a mix of action, comedy, romance and drama), with famous extra-large samosas available in the interval. All films are in Hindi only, though. (☏011-23272903; 4/1 Asaf Ali Rd; Ⓜ New Delhi)

Shopping

Chandni Chowk   CLOTHING, ELECTRONICS

29 Ⓐ MAP P42, E3

Old Delhi's backbone is an iconic shopping strip, dotted by temples, snarled by traffic and crammed with stores selling everything from street food to saris. Tiny bazaars lead off the main drag, so you can explore these small lanes, which glitter with jewellery, decorations, paper goods and more. (◷10am-7pm; Ⓜ Chandni Chowk)

Kinari Bazaar   MARKET

30 Ⓐ MAP P42, E3

Kinari means 'hem' in Hindi, and this colour-blazing market sells all the trimmings that finish off an outfit. It's famous for *zardozi* (gold embroidery), temple trim and wedding turbans, and is extremely photogenic. (Kinari Bazaar; ⏰11am-8pm; Ⓜ Jama Masjid)

Ballimaran

MARKET

31 🔒 MAP P42, D3

This area is apparently where Delhi's Yamuna boat operators once lived. Today this market street and the smaller lanes fanning off it specialise in sequined slippers and fancy, curly-toed jootis (traditional slip-on shoes). (Ballimaran; ⏰10am-8pm; Ⓜ Chandni Chowk)

Dariba Kalan

MARKET

32 🔒 MAP P42, F3

For silver (jewellery, ornaments, old coins), head for Dariba Kalan,

the alley near the Sisganj Gurdwara, and with the easy-to-spot Jalebi Wala (p47) at its mouth. (⏰10am-8pm; Ⓜ Lal Qila)

Nai Sarak

MARKET

33 🔒 MAP P42, E3

Running south from the old Town Hall, Nai Sarak is lined with stalls selling saris, shawls, chiffon and *lehenga* (blouse and skirt combo). (⏰10am-8pm; Ⓜ Jama Masjid)

Spice Market

MARKET

34 🔒 MAP P42, D3

It feels as if little has changed for centuries in Delhi's fabulously atmospheric, labyrinthine spice market, as labourers hustle through the narrow lanes with huge packages of herbs and spices on their heads

Spice Market

Old Delhi (Shahjahanabad) Shopping

whilst sunlight pours down through cracks in the hessian sacks hanging overhead for shade. The colours are wonderful – red chillies, yellow turmeric, green cardamons – and there's so much spice in the air, people walk around unable to suppress their sneezes. (Gadodia Market; Khari Baoli; ⓂChandni Chowk)

Aap Ki Pasand
DRINKS

35 🔒 MAP P42, G5

Specialists in the finest Indian teas, from Darjeeling and Assam to Nilgiri and Kangra. You can try before you buy, and teas come lovingly packaged in drawstring bags. There's another branch at Santushti Shopping Complex (p91). (San-Cha Tea; 📞23260373; www.aapkipasandtea.com; 15 Netaji Subhash Marg; ⏱10am-7pm Mon-Sat; ⓂJama Masjid, Delhi Gate)

Shopping for Tabla

As well as the many shops and markets to explore in Old Delhi, it's worth browsing the myriad **musical instrument shops** (Map p42, G5; Netaji Subhash Marg; ⏱10am-8pm Mon-Sat; ⓂDelhi Gate, Jama Masjid) along Netaji Subhash Marg for sitars, tabla sets and other beautifully crafted Indian instruments. Expect to pay upwards of ₹20,000 for a decent quality sitar, and around ₹3000 to ₹6000 for a tabla pair.

Main Bazaar
HANDICRAFTS, CLOTHING

36 🔒 MAP P42, B6

Backpacker Central, this crazy-busy bazaar that runs through Paharganj sells almost everything you want, and a whole lot more. It's great for buying presents, clothes, inexpensive jewellery bits and bobs, and luggage to put everything in as you're leaving India, or for hippy-dippy clothes to wear on your trip. Haggle with purpose. (Paharganj; ⏱10am-9pm Tue-Sun; ⓂRamakrishna Ashram Marg)

Yes Helping Hands
CLOTHING

37 🔒 MAP P42, A6

With its roots in Pokhara, Nepal, this fair-trade nonprofit organisation sells quality weave and knitwear, including pashmina shawls, cashmere scarfs and hemp bags with an aim to helping provide training and employment opportunities for people with disabilities in Nepal and Ladakh. (www.yeshelpinghands.org; Main Bazaar, Paharganj; ⏱9am-9pm; ⓂRamakrishna Ashram Marg)

Daryaganj Kitab Bazaar
MARKET

38 🔒 MAP P42, F6

Come Sunday, second-hand books spread along the pavement for around 1km from Delhi Gate westwards along Asaf Ali Rd. Rummage for everything from Mills & Boon to vintage children's books. Many books are sold by weight, for as little as ₹20 per kg. It's best to arrive early (before 9am), as it gets busy.

Daryaganj Kitab Bazaar

(Book Market; Asaf Ali Rd; ⊙8am-6pm Sun; Ⓜ Delhi Gate)

Delhi Foundation of Deaf Women
ARTS & CRAFTS

39 🔒 MAP P42, B6

Beautiful handmade handicrafts (bags, purses, gift cards, bookmarks) made by members of the city's deaf foundation and sold from their community hall. Very hard to find; from Main Bazaar, walk up Chandi Wali Gali, turn right at the end, and it's soon on your right, down a tiny alley. (DFDW; www. dfdw.net; 1st fl, DDA Community Hall, Mantola Mohalla, near Chandi Wali Gali, Paharganj; ⊙10am-6pm Mon-Sat; Ⓜ Ramakrishna Ashram Marg)

Paharganj Vegetable & Spice Market
MARKET

40 🔒 MAP P42, B6

This long side street is where Paharganj locals buy their veg, but it's also the best (and cheapest) place round here for spices – 100g bags of cumin or coriander will only set you back ₹20 or ₹25. (⊙8am-10pm; Ⓜ Ramakrishna Ashram Marg)

Paharganj Fruit Market
MARKET

41 🔒 MAP P42, B6

South of Main Bazaar, fruit-stall sellers punt their wares well into the evening. (⊙8am-10pm; Ⓜ Ramakrishna Ashram Marg)

Explore ⊕
New Delhi

Welcome to the British Raj. New Delhi was designed on an imperial scale after George V decided to move the capital of British India from Calcutta to here in 1911. Much of its grandeur remains today, including the circular, colonnaded shopping precinct Connaught Place, the imposing government buildings that look out along Rajpath, and the rambling colonial-era bungalows, some of which now house museums.

The Short List

○ **Rajpath (p58)** *Joining hundreds of domestic tourists on a pleasant early-evening stroll along this grand parade, from the President's House to iconic India Gate.*

○ **Connaught Place (p64)** *Dodging persistent touts as you hop from shop to shop at New Delhi's confusingly circular, British-era shopping precinct.*

○ **National Museum (p64)** *Picking your way through centuries of Indian history at Delhi's best museum.*

○ **Gurdwara Bangla Sahib (p64)** *Being welcomed with open arms into Delhi's largest and most important Sikh temple.*

○ **Agrasen ki Baoli (p65)** *Escaping the city for a moment of quiet reflection in this hauntingly beautiful, ancient step-well.*

Getting There & Around

Ⓜ Connaught Place's metro station is called Rajiv Chowk.

Autorickshaws Some sights in New Delhi are slightly beyond the reach of the metro.

Cycle-rickshaws Banned from Connaught Place, and much of Rajpath, but still good for short hops.

Neighbourhood Map on p62

Connaught Place (p64) JAYANT BAHEL/SHUTTERSTOCK ©

Top Sight 📷
Rajpath

Rajpath (Kingsway) is a vast parade linking India Gate to the offices of the Indian government. Built on an imperial scale between 1914 and 1931, it was designed by Edwin Lutyens and Herbert Baker, and underlined the ascendance of the British rulers. Yet just 16 years later, the Brits were out on their ear and Indian politicians were pacing the corridors of power.

◎ MAP P62, D6

Ⓜ Central Secretariat

Western End

At the western end of Rajpath, **Rashtrapati Bhavan** (President's House; 📞 011-23015321; www.rashtrapatisachivalaya.gov.in/rbtour; Rajpath; ₹50; 🕙9am-4pm Fri-Sun, online reservation required), the official residence of the president of India, is now partially open to the public via guided tours. It is fronted by the dome-crowned, twin buildings of **North Secretariat** and **South Secretariat**, which house government ministries. They aren't open to the public, though they are lit up attractively at night. The Indian parliament meets nearby at the **Sansad Bhavan** (Parliament House; Sansad Marg), a circular, colonnaded edifice, also not open to the public.

How to visit Rashtrapati Bhavan

Tours of Rashtrapati Bhavan are only available at weekends, and you must pre-book and pay for them online at www.rashtrapatisachivalaya.gov.in/rbtour. Places are limited, so it's wise to book at least one or two weeks in advance. Tours of Rashtrapati Bhavan's museum and Mughal gardens also need to be booked in the same way.

Eastern End

At Rajpath's eastern end is mighty India Gate (p65), a 42m-high stone memorial arch, which pays tribute to the 90,000 Indian Army soldiers who died in WWI, the Northwest Frontier operations and the 1919 Anglo-Afghan War.

Rajpath Park

An elongated park, popular with picnicking families and containing a slim boating canal, runs along both sides of Rajpath, and offers some tree-shaded respite on hot days.

★ Top Tips

⚬ Save your stroll along Rajpath until the relative cool of the late afternoon, when street-food vendors arrive.

⚬ Rashtrapati Bhavan's Mughal Gardens are only open from mid-February to mid-March, when they are in full bloom, but are well worth seeing if you're in Delhi at this time.

✖ Take a Break

There are no shops or restaurants on Rajpath itself, but this is good picnic territory, and street-food vendors pop up late afternoon, especially near India Gate. Alternatively, grab a snack or a cheap lunch in the National Museum's no-frills **cafe** (Map p62, D6, Janpath; snacks & dishes ₹20-100; 🕙9am-6pm; Ⓜ️Udyog Bhawan); no need to pay the museum entrance fee.

Walking Tour 🚶

Lutyens' New Delhi

Sir Edwin Landseer Lutyens (1869–1944) played an instrumental role in designing and building New Delhi, and this walk takes you past some of the city's best-known Raj-era buildings, culminating in a stroll along the wide, park-lined avenue of Rajpath that ends at Delhi's iconic India Gate.

Walk Facts

Start Connaught Place;
Ⓜ Rajiv Chowk (Connaught Place)

End India Gate;
Ⓜ Central Secretariat

Length 5.5km; three to four hours

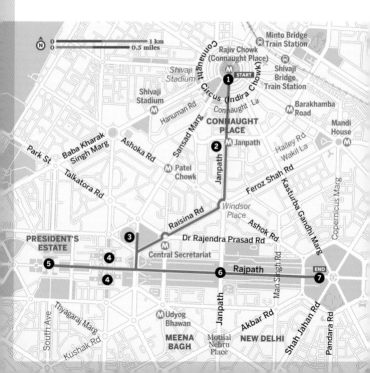

❶ Connaught Place

Begin your walk at Connaught Place (p64), the confusing circular shopping district that was named after George V's uncle, the Duke of Connaught, and fashioned after the Palladian colonnades of Bath. The greying, whitewashed, colonnaded streets radiate out from the central circle of Rajiv Chowk; you want to aim for F-Block, before walking south down Janpath.

❷ The Imperial

Before long, you'll reach the splendid Raj-era hotel, the Imperial, built in 1931. Its classicism-meets-art-deco design was the work of one of Lutyens' associates, FB Blomfield. For an extra touch of British Raj, time your visit to take in high tea at the Atrium (p70).

❸ Sansad Bhavan

Continue south to Windsor Place roundabout and take the second right (Raisina Rd) to the next roundabout. Go straight to reach a fountain, where Sansad Bhavan (p59) will be to your right. This circular, colonnaded building, designed by Lutyens and Herbert Baker, was where the 1947 handover of power from Britain to newly independent India took place. Parliament meets here.

❹ North & South Secretariat Buildings

Turn left to reach the grand avenue known as Rajpath, where you'll spot India Gate off to your left. Before that, though, turn right, and climb the slope to the twin government buildings of North Secretariat (p59) and South Secretariat (p59), both of which were designed by Baker in 1912, and are lit up in the evening.

❺ Rashtrapati Bhavan

Directly ahead of you are the grounds of Rashtrapati Bhavan (p59), formerly home to the British Viceroy, and now the official residence of the president of India. If you've booked a tour online, show them your confirmation slip at the gate. Otherwise, make an about turn and begin your long march east along Rajpath.

❻ Rajpath

Known as Kingsway in British times, Rajpath (p58) is a wide avenue linking Rashtrapati Bhavan and India Gate. It was built as a parade ground on an imperial scale and is flanked by elongated parks with waterways that are popular local hangouts and offer pleasant tree-shaded respite on hot days.

❼ India Gate

At the far end of Rajpath you'll reach India Gate (p65), Delhi's iconic 42m-tall war-memorial archway designed by Lutyens in 1921. There's a constant buzz of activity, street-food sellers and other hawkers here, particularly in late afternoon.

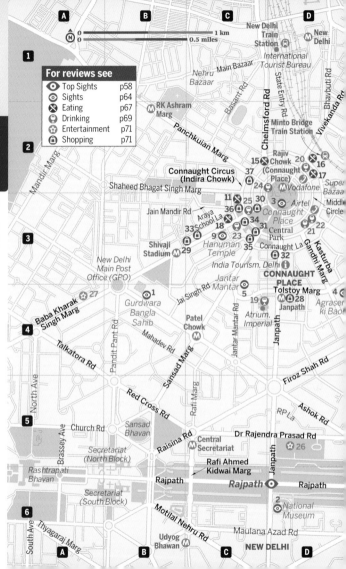

New Delhi

For reviews see
- ◉ Top Sights — p58
- ● Sights — p64
- ✖ Eating — p67
- ☕ Drinking — p69
- ☆ Entertainment — p71
- 🔒 Shopping — p71

New Delhi Train Station

New Delhi

International Tourist Bureau

Nehru Bazaar

Main Bazaar

RK Ashram Marg

Basant Rd

Chelmsford Rd

State Entry Rd

Minto Bridge Train Station

Vivekanda Rd

Bhawbuti Rd

Panchkuian Marg

Mandir Marg

Rajiv Chowk 20 16
15 Chowk (Connaught Place) 17

Super Bazaa

Connaught Circus (Indira Chowk)

37

24 Vodafone

Shaheed Bhagat Singh Marg

11 25 30

Middle Circle

Jain Mandir Rd

Araya School La

36

3 Airtel

9 23

18

Connaught Place

33

34

31

22

Shivaji Stadium

29

Hanuman Temple

35 Central Park

Connaught La

32

21

Kasturba Gandhi Marg

New Delhi Main Post Office (GPO)

India Tourism, Delhi

CONNAUGHT PLACE

Jantar Mantar

Baba Kharak Singh Marg

27

1

Gurdwara Bangla Sahib

Jai Singh Rd

5

Tolstoy Marg

19 28 Janpath

4

Agrasen ki Baoli

Talkatora Rd

Pandit Pant Rd

Mahadev Rd

Patel Chowk

Jantar Mantar Rd

Atrium, Imperial

Janpath

North Ave

Church Rd

Sansad Marg

Rafi Marg

Firoz Shah Rd

Red Cross Rd

Brassey Ave

Sansad Bhavan

Raisina Rd

Central Secretariat

Dr Rajendra Prasad Rd

Ashok Rd

RP La

Secretariat (North Block)

Rajpath

Rafi Ahmed Kidwai Marg

26

Rashtrapati Bhavan

Secretariat (South Block)

Motilal Nehru Rd

Rajpath

Rajpath

Janpath

2

National Museum

Thyagaraj Marg

South Ave

Udyog Bhavan

Maulana Azad Rd

NEW DELHI

0 — 1 km
0 — 0.5 miles

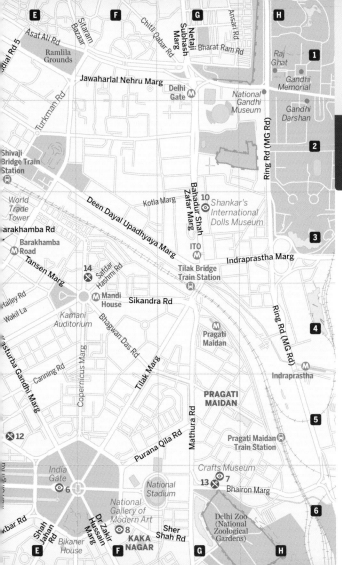

New Delhi

E F G H

Asaf Ali Rd
Ramlila Grounds
Sitaram Bazaar
Chitli Qabar Rd
Netaji Subhash Marg
Ansari Rd
Bharat Ram Rd

1 Raj Ghat
Gandhi Memorial

Jawaharlal Nehru Marg

Turkman Rd
Delhi Gate

National Gandhi Museum
Gandhi Darshan

2

Shivaji Bridge Train Station

Ring Rd (MG Rd)

World Trade Tower

Deen Dayal Upadhyaya Marg

Kotla Marg

Bahadur Shah Zafar Marg

10 Shankar's International Dolls Museum

3

Barakhamba Rd
Barakhamba Road
Tansen Marg

ITO

Saftar Hashmi Rd

Indraprastha Marg

Tilak Bridge Train Station

14

Hailey Rd
Wakil La
Mandi House
Sikandra Rd

Kamani Auditorium

Bhagwan Das Rd

Pragati Maidan

Ring Rd (MG Rd)

4

Copernicus Marg
Canning Rd
Tilak Marg

Indraprastha

Kasturba Gandhi Marg

PRAGATI MAIDAN

5

12

Purana Qila Rd

Mathura Rd

Pragati Maidan Train Station

India Gate
6

National Stadium

Crafts Museum
13 **7**

Bhairon Marg

6

Akbar Rd
Shah Jahan Rd
Dr Zakir Hussain Marg

National Gallery of Modern Art

8

Bikaner House

KAKA NAGAR

Sher Shah Rd

Delhi Zoo (National Zoological Gardens)

E F G H

Sights

Gurdwara Bangla Sahib

SIKH TEMPLE

1 MAP P62, B4

This magnificent white-marble gurdwara (Sikh temple), topped by glinting golden onion domes, was constructed at the site where the eighth Sikh guru, Harkrishan Dev, stayed before his 1664 death. Despite his tender years, the six-year-old guru tended to victims of Delhi's cholera and smallpox epidemic, and the waters of the large tank are said to have healing powers. It's full of colour and life, yet tranquil, and live devotional songs waft over the compound. (Ashoka Rd; ⏱4am-9pm; Ⓜ Patel Chowk)

Changing of the Guard

Members of the public can make a rare foray into the forecourt of Rashtrapati Bhavan (p59) to witness the twice-weekly Changing of the Guard ceremony. It's held at 8am on Saturdays (10am mid-March to mid-November) and at 4.30pm on Sundays (5.30pm mid-March to mid-November) and lasts around 45 minutes. Entry is via Gate 2 or Gate 37. Numbers are limited. Bring your passport.

National Museum

MUSEUM

2 MAP P62, D6

This glorious, if dusty, museum is full of treasures. Mind-bogglingly ancient, sophisticated figurines from the Harappan civilisation, almost 5000 years old, include the remarkable *Dancing Girl*, and there are also some fine ceramics from the even-older Nal civilisation. Other items include Buddha relics, exquisite jewellery, miniature paintings, medieval woodcarvings, textiles and musical instruments. Don't miss the immense, five-tier wooden temple chariot built in South India in the 19th century. (☏011-23019272; www.national museumindia.gov.in; Janpath; Indian/foreigner ₹20/650, camera ₹20/300; ⏱10am-6pm Tue-Sun, free guided tour 10.30am & 2.30pm Tue-Fri, 10.30am, 11.30am, 2.30pm & 3pm Sat & Sun; Ⓜ Udyog Bhawan)

Connaught Place

AREA

3 MAP P62, D3

This confusing circular shopping district was named after George V's uncle, the Duke of Connaught, and fashioned after the Palladian colonnades of Bath. Greying, whitewashed, colonnaded streets radiate out from the central circle of Rajiv Chowk, with blocks G to N in the outer circle and A to F in the inner circle. Today they mainly harbour brash, largely interchangeable but popular, bars, and international chain stores, plus a few good hotels and restaurants. Touts are rampant. (Ⓜ Rajiv Chowk)

New Delhi Sights

Gurdwara Bangla Sahib

Agrasen ki Baoli
MONUMENT

4 ⊙ MAP P62, D4

This atmospheric 14th-century step-well was once set in the countryside, till the city grew up around it; 103 steps descend to the bottom, flanked by arched niches. It's a remarkable thing to discover among the office towers southeast of Connaught Place. It's garnered more attention since it was used as a shelter by Aamir Khan in the 2015 movie *PK*. (Hailey Lane; ⊙dawn–dusk; Ⓜ Janpath)

Jantar Mantar
HISTORIC SITE

5 ⊙ MAP P62, C4

This is one of five observatories built by Maharaja Jai Singh II, ruler of Jaipur. Constructed in 1725, Jantar Mantar (derived from the Sanskrit word for 'instrument', but which has also become the Hindi word for 'abracadabra') is a quiet park containing a collection of curving geometric buildings that are carefully calibrated to monitor the movement of the stars and planets. (Sansad Marg; Indian/foreigner ₹25/300, video ₹25; ⊙dawn–dusk; Ⓜ Patel Chowk)

India Gate
MONUMENT

6 ⊙ MAP P62, E6

Designed by Lutyens in 1921, this imposing 42m-high stone memorial arch pays tribute to around 90,000 Indian Army soldiers who died in WWI, the Northwest Frontier operations and the 1919 Anglo-Afghan War. The *chhatri* behind it contained a statue of George V, later moved to

Coronation Park. The arch has a constant buzz of tourists, *budhdhi ke bal* ('old lady's hair' – candy-floss) sellers and other hawkers. (Rajpath; ⏰24hr; Ⓜ Central Secretariat)

Crafts Museum
MUSEUM

7 ◉ MAP P62, G6

Much of this lovely museum is outside, including tree-shaded carvings and life-size examples of village huts from various regions of India. Displays celebrate the traditional crafts of India, with some beautiful textiles on display indoors, such as examples of embroidery from Kashmir and cross-stitch from Punjab. Highlights include a huge wooden 18th-century temple chariot from Maharashtra. Artisans sell their products in the rear courtyard. The museum also includes the excellent Cafe Lota and a very good shop. (☎011-23371641; Bhairon Marg; Indian/foreigner ₹20/200; ⏰10am-5pm Tue-Sun; Ⓜ Pragati Maidan)

National Gallery of Modern Art
GALLERY

8 ◉ MAP P62, F6

Housed in the Maharaja of Jaipur's domed former palace (built in 1936), Delhi's flagship art gallery displays collections tracing the development of Indian art from the mid-19th century to the present day, from 'Company Paintings' created by Indian artists to please their British rulers to the artworks of Nobel Prize–winner Rabindranath Tagore. Photography

---

Appreciating Mahatma Gandhi

The New Delhi neighbourhood is dotted with sights dedicated to the late, great, Indian Independence leader Mahatma Gandhi. The house where he spent his final days before being assassinated in 1948 is now a peaceful museum called **Gandhi Smriti** (☎011-23012843; 5 Tees Jan Marg; admission free; ⏰10am-5pm Tue-Sun, closed 2nd Sat of month; Ⓜ Lok Kalyan Marg).

Close to the Yamuna River is a further cluster of sights dedicated to Gandhi, including the **Gandhi Memorial** (Map p62, H1; Raj Ghat; Ⓜ Jama Masjid), where he was cremated, and the **National Gandhi Museum** (Map p62, H1; ☎011-23310168; http://gandhi museum.org; Raj Ghat; admission free; ⏰9.30am-5.30pm Tue-Sun; Ⓜ Jama Masjid).

Located within peaceful, landscaped gardens, **Gandhi Darshan** (Map p62, H2; Kisan Ghat Rd; admission free; ⏰10am-5pm Mon-Sat; Ⓜ Indraprastha) displays some interesting photos and paintings documenting the life of Gandhi.

is prohibited. (☎011-23386111; www.
ngmaindia.gov.in; Jaipur House, Dr
Zakir Hussain Marg; Indian/foreigner
₹20/500; ⏱11am-6.30pm Tue-Sun;
Ⓜ Khan Market)

Hanuman Temple

HINDU TEMPLE

9 ◉ MAP P62, C3

This popular Hindu temple is
dedicated to the much-revered
god Hanuman, sometimes referred
to as the Monkey God. It throngs
with devotees on Tuesdays and
Saturdays, and is usually busy
with visiting monkeys too, who
hang around outside waiting to be
fed. Unusually, the temple has a
crescent moon (usually an Islamic
symbol) fixed to its *sikhara* (spire).
(Hanuman Mandir; Baba Kharak Singh
Rd, Connaught Place; ⏱dawn-dusk;
Ⓜ Rajiv Chowk)

Shankar's International Dolls Museum

MUSEUM

10 ◉ MAP P62, G3

Set up by K Shankar Pillai
(1902–89), a renowned political
cartoonist, who started collecting
dolls in 1950 after he was given
one as a gift from the Hungarian
ambassador, this museum, right
beside ITO metro station, has an
impressive if quirky collection of
more than 7000 costumed dolls
from 85 countries. (☎011-3316970;
www.childrensbooktrust.com; Nehru
House, 4 Bahadur Shah Zafar Marg;
adult/child ₹30/12; ⏱10am-6pm Tue-
Sun; Ⓜ ITO)

Eating

Hotel Saravana Bhavan

SOUTH INDIAN $$

11 🍴 MAP P62, C3

Delhi's best thali (₹230 to ₹320)
is served up in unassuming
surroundings – a simple Tamil
canteen on the edge of Connaught
Place. There are queues every
meal time to sample the splendid
array of richly spiced veg curries,
dips, breads and condiments that
make it onto every thali plate. The
dosa are very popular too. (15 P-
Block, Connaught Place; dishes ₹120-
290; ⏱8am-11pm; Ⓜ Rajiv Chowk)

Andhra Pradesh Bhawan Canteen

SOUTH INDIAN $

12 🍴 MAP P62, E5

A hallowed bargain, the canteen
at the Andhra Pradesh state
house serves cheap and delicious
unlimited South Indian thalis to
a seemingly unlimited stream
of patrons. Come on Sunday for
the fabled Hyderabadi chicken
biryani (₹235). (1 Ashoka Rd; dishes
₹150-180, thalis ₹130, breakfast ₹75;
⏱8-10.30am, noon-3pm & 7.30-10pm;
Ⓜ Patel Chowk)

Cafe Lota

MODERN INDIAN $$

13 🍴 MAP P62, G6

Bamboo slices the sunlight into
flattering stripes at this outdoor
restaurant offering a modern take
on delicious Indian cooking from
across the regions. Sample its
take on fish and (sweet potato)

chips, or *palak patta chaat* (crispy spinach, potatoes and chick-peas with spiced yoghurt and chutneys), as well as amazing desserts and breakfasts. It's great for kids. (Crafts Museum; dishes ₹215-415; ⏱8am-9.30pm; Ⓜ Pragati Maidan)

Triveni Terrace Cafe
CAFE $

14 ✕ MAP P62, F3

Located in a peaceful garden-courtyard inside Triveni Art Gallery, this delightful cafe has seating on a plant-filled terrace overlooking a small, grassy amphi-theatre, where dance rehearsals sometimes take place while you eat. The small menu includes tasty, good-value Indian meals and snacks (*pakora*, *paratha*, thali) plus toasted sandwiches and French-press coffee (₹120). (205 Tansen Marg, Mandi House; dishes ₹70-200; ⏱10am-9pm, food to 6.30pm; Ⓜ Mandi House)

Véda
INDIAN $$$

15 ✕ MAP P62, C2

Fashion designer Rohit Baal created Véda's sumptuous interior, making for Connaught Place's most dimly lit eatery, a dark boudoir with swirling neo-Murano chandeliers and shimmering mirror mosaics. The menu proffers tasty classic Mughlai dishes (butter chicken, dhal makhani and the like) and it mixes a mean martini. (☎011-41513535; 27 H-Block, Connaught Place; mains ₹500-700; ⏱noon-11.30pm; Ⓜ Rajiv Chowk)

Kake-da-Hotel
MUGHLAI $

16 ✕ MAP P62, D2

This no-frills, always-busy *dhaba* (snack bar) is a basic hole in the wall that's hugely popular with local workers for its famous butter chicken (₹230) and other Mughlai Punjabi dishes. Staff are rushed off their feet, but the owner is welcoming to the few foreign diners who visit. (☎9136666820;

Home-cooked Meals

The online foodie community **Traveling Spoon** (www.travelingspoon.com) connects locals with travellers wishing to experience home-made meals. Foodie travellers can choose from a clutch of hosts happy to cook, teach and serve traditional cuisine from the comfort of their homes. To find hosts, search for New Delhi on the website; prices depend on the host and meal served.

Eat With India (www.eatwithindia.com) is a similar idea, bringing foodies and culinary experts together for pop-up dinners over multi-course meals in private homes across India.

Véda

67 Municipal Market; mains ₹90-300; ⊙noon-11.30pm; Ⓜ Rajiv Chowk)

Naturals ICE CREAM $

17 ✘ MAP P62, D2

Founder Mr Kamath's dad was a mango vendor in Mangalore, which apparently inspired his love of fruit. He went on to start Naturals, with its wonderfully creamy, fresh flavours, such as watermelon, coconut, (heavenly) mango and roasted almond. (8 L-Block, Connaught Place; single scoop ₹70; ⊙11am-midnight; Ⓜ Rajiv Chowk)

Coffee Home INDIAN $

18 ✘ MAP P62, C3

Shaded under the wide reaches of an old banyan tree, the garden courtyard at Coffee Home is always busy with office workers lingering over chai and feasting on South Indian snacks such as masala dosa. It is handily located next to the government emporiums. (Baba Kharak Singh Marg; dishes ₹50-150; ⊙11am-8pm; Ⓜ Shivaji Stadium)

Drinking

1911 BAR

19 🍷 MAP P62, C4

The Imperial, built in the 1930s, resonates with bygone splendour. This bar is a more recent addition, but still riffs on the Raj. Here you can sip the perfect cocktail (₹1000) amid designer-clad clientele, against a backdrop of faded photos and murals of maharajas. (Imperial Hotel, Janpath; ⊙11am-12.45am; Ⓜ Janpath)

Unplugged

BAR

20 MAP P62, D2

There's nowhere else like this in Connaught Place. You could forget you were in CP, in fact, with the big courtyard garden, wrought-iron chairs and tables, and swing seats, all under the shade of a banyan tree hung with basket-weave lanterns. There's live music on Wednesday, Friday, Saturday and Sunday evenings: anything from alt-rock to electro-fusion. (☎011-33107701; 23 L-Block, Connaught Place; beers/cocktails from ₹145/400; ⏰noon-midnight; Ⓜ Rajiv Chowk)

Chai Point

CAFE

21 MAP P62, D3

This buzzing, split-level cafe specialises in healthy chai infusions (masala, ginger, cardamom, lemongrass; ₹75 to ₹100) but also serves good lassis (₹119 to ₹129) and fresh coffee alongside banana cake and other sweet treats. Ask for a glass cup; otherwise you'll get your chai in a less-than-satisfying disposable paper cup. (N-Block, Connaught Place; ⏰8am-11pm; 🛜; Ⓜ Rajiv Chowk)

Cha Bar

CAFE

22 MAP P62, D3

Connaught Place's Oxford Bookstore contains the hugely popular cafe Cha Bar, with more than 150 types of tea to choose from, as well as a good-value food menu including a range of tasty biryanis (₹170). At lunchtimes it buzzes with happy, chattering, 20-something locals. (Oxford Bookstore, 81 N-Block, Connaught Place; tea ₹35-100, dishes ₹100-175; ⏰9.30am-9.30pm; Ⓜ Rajiv Chowk)

Indian Coffee House

CAFE

23 MAP P62, C3

Up on the 2nd floor of Mohan Singh Place, Indian Coffee House has faded-to-the-point-of-dilapidated charm, with the waiters' plummage-like hats and uniforms giving them a rakish swagger. You can feast on finger chips and South Indian snacks like it's 1952, and the roof terrace is a tranquil spot to linger, although watch out for marauding macaques! (2nd fl, Mohan Singh Place, Baba Kharak Singh Marg; snacks ₹50-100, filter coffee ₹36; ⏰9am-9pm; Ⓜ Rajiv Chowk)

High Tea at the Imperial

Can there be anything more genteel than high tea at the Imperial? Sip Darjeeling's finest from bone-china cups and pluck dainty sandwiches and cakes from tiered stands, while discussing the latest goings-on in Shimla and Dalhousie. High tea is served in the **Atrium** (Map p62, C4; Imperial Hotel, Janpath; ⏰8am-11.30pm; Ⓜ Janpath) from 3pm to 6pm daily (₹1500 plus tax).

Keventer's Milkshakes CAFE

24 MAP P62, D2

Keventer's has a cult following for its legendary creamy milkshakes (₹80), slurped out of milk bottles on the pavement in front of the stand. (17 A-Block, Connaught Place; 9am-11pm; Rajiv Chowk)

Lord of the Drinks BAR

25 MAP P62, C3

A cavernous space done up in wood, leather and metal trim, with cosy corners and a huge sports TV screen. Serves trademark oversized drinks, including mugs of Kingfisher for ₹135, while everything goes on the food menu, from *bhurji* (crumbled spiced paneer) to Parmesan tart. (9999827155, 9999827144; G-72, 1st fl, Outer Circle, Connaught Place; beers/cocktails from ₹135/545, mains ₹400-800; 11am-1am; ; Rajiv Chowk)

Entertainment

Indira Gandhi National Centre for the Arts ARTS CENTRE

26 MAP P62, D5

A hub of cultural and artsy seminars, exhibitions and performances housed in a well-located, landscaped sprawl not far from India Gate. Frequented by culture vultures for a regular fix of classical and vocal recitals, dance performances, film screenings and literary fests. See the website for forthcoming events and activities. (011-23388105; www.ignca.gov.in;

11 Mansingh Rd, near Andhra Bhavan; 9am-5.30pm Mon-Fri; Janpath, Central Secretariat, Patel Chowk)

Akshara Theatre THEATRE

27 MAP P62, A4

Small, but well regarded theatre with frequent shows. Puts on its own small-scale drama productions, but also often hosts comedy nights. (011-23361075; www.aksharatheatre.com; 11-B Baba Kharak Singh Marg, beside RML Hospital; tickets from ₹200; Shivaji Stadium, Patel Chowk)

Shopping

Central Cottage Industries Emporium CRAFTS

28 MAP P62, D4

This government-run multilevel store is a wonderful treasure trove of fixed-price, India-wide handicrafts. Prices are higher than in the state emporiums, but the selection of woodcarvings, jewellery, pottery, papier mâché, stationery, brassware, textiles (including shawls), toys, rugs, beauty products and miniature paintings makes it a glorious one-stop shop for beautiful crafts. (011-23326790; Janpath; 10am-7pm; Janpath)

Kamala ARTS & CRAFTS

29 MAP P62, C3

Crafts, curios, textiles and homewares from the Crafts Council of India, designed with flair and using traditional techniques but offering some contemporary, out-of-the-ordinary designs. (Baba Kharak Singh Marg; ⏰10am-7pm Mon-Sat; Ⓜ️Rajiv Chowk)

Fabindia

CLOTHING, HOMEWARES

30 🔒 MAP P62, C3

Surprisingly well-priced, high-quality, ready-made clothes in funky Indian fabrics, from elegant kurtas (long collarless shirts) and dupattas (women's scarves) to Western-style shirts, plus stylish homewares. (www.fabindia.com; 1 A-Block, Connaught Place; ⏰10am-8.30pm; Ⓜ️Rajiv Chowk)

The Shop

CLOTHING, HOMEWARES

31 🔒 MAP P62, C3

Gorgeous little boutique with a calm, no-pressure-to-buy ambience, attractive Indian clothing,

and light, bright printed-cotton homewares. (10 Regal Bldg, Sansad Marg; ⏰9.30am-7.30pm Mon-Sat, 11am-6pm Sun; Ⓜ️Janpath, Rajiv Chowk)

Janpath & Tibetan Markets

ARTS & CRAFTS

32 🔒 MAP P62, D3

These twin markets, made up of small shopfronts stretching along Janpath, sell shimmering mirrorwork embroidery, colourful shawls, Tibetan bric-a-brac, brass Oms, dangly earrings and lots of clothing. There are some good finds if you rummage through the junk, and if you haggle you can get some bargains. (Janpath; ⏰11.30am-7pm Mon-Sat; Ⓜ️Rajiv Chowk)

Mahatma Gandhi's Cloth

More than 80 years ago, Gandhi urged Indians to support the freedom movement by getting rid of their foreign-made clothing and turning to *khadi* – homespun cloth. *Khadi* became a symbol of Indian independence, and the fabric is still associated with politics. The government-run, nonprofit group Khadi and Village Industries Commission (www.kvic.org.in) serves to promote *khadi,* which is usually cotton, but can also be silk or wool.

Khadi outlets are simple, no-nonsense places, where you can pick up genuine Indian clothing such as kurta pyjamas, scarves, saris and, at some branches, assorted handicrafts – you will find them all over India, including a large outlet called Khadi Gramodyog Bhawan located in Connaught Place. Prices are reasonable and are often discounted in the period around Gandhi's birthday (2 October). A number of outlets also have a tailoring service on offer.

State Emporiums HANDICRAFTS, CLOTHING

33 🔒 MAP P62, C3

Handily in a row are these regional treasure-filled emporiums. They may have the air of torpor that often afflicts governmental enterprises, but shopping here is like travelling around India – top stops include Kashmir, for papier mâché and carpets; Rajasthan, for miniature paintings and puppets; Uttar Pradesh, for marble inlay work; Karnataka, for sandalwood sculptures; and Odisha, for stone carvings. (Baba Kharak Singh Marg; ⏰11am-1.30pm & 2-6.30pm Mon-Sat; Ⓜ Shivaji Stadium)

Khadi Gramodyog Bhawan CLOTHING

34 🔒 MAP P62, C3

Known for its excellent *khadi* (homespun cloth), including good-value shawls, *salwar kameez* and *kurta pyjama,* this three-floor shop also sells handmade paper, incense, spices, henna and lovely natural soaps. (Regal Bldg, 24 Connaught Circus; ⏰11am-7.30pm; Ⓜ Rajiv Chowk)

People Tree HANDICRAFTS, CLOTHING

35 🔒 MAP P62, C3

This hole-in-the-wall shop sells fixed-price, fair-trade T-shirts with funky Indian designs and urban attitude, as well as bags, jewellery and Indian-god cushions. (Regal Bldg, Sansad Marg; ⏰11.30am-7.30pm; Ⓜ Rajiv Chowk)

Nalli Silk Sarees CLOTHING

36 🔒 MAP P62, C3

Founded in Southern India in 1928, this venerable sari shop offers a rainbow palette of silk and cotton saris. (7/90 P-Block, Connaught Place; ⏰10am-8.30pm; Ⓜ Rajiv Chowk)

Rikhi Ram MUSIC

37 🔒 MAP P62, C2

A tiny, but beautiful, old shop selling professional classic and electric sitars, tablas and more. Tablas start at ₹50,000. (📞011-23327685; www.rikhiram.com; 8A G-Block, Connaught Place; ⏰11am-8pm Mon-Sat; Ⓜ Rajiv Chowk)

Explore ✦

Sunder Nagar, Nizamuddin & Lodi Colony

This sweeping neighbourhood acts as a wide, but shallow buffer between the city centre and South Delhi proper. Its sights are scattered far and wide, so visiting them requires some planning, but this area, and particularly its eastern half, is well worth delving into; it hides some of Delhi's top-draw archaeological sites as well as some standout street markets.

The Short List

○ **Humayun's Tomb (p78)** Sizing up the beautifully proportioned Mughal tomb, said to have been the inspiration for the Taj Mahal.

○ **Purana Qila (p76)** Exploring the ruined ramparts and landscaped gardens of Delhi's magnificent Old Fort.

○ **Hazrat Nizam-ud-din Dargah (p80)** Being swept up in the spiritual fervour that radiates out from this holy Muslim shrine.

○ **Lodi Garden (p83)** Picnicking on the lawns, walking through the bamboo groves and marvelling at the 15th-century tombs inside Delhi's loveliest park.

Getting There & Around

Ⓜ Most sights are close to a metro station, though some stations may leave you 1km or 2km short.

Autorickshaw These will help with the final push from your metro station to the sight you're aiming for.

🚗 The transport of choice in the diplomatic enclave.

Neighbourhood Map on p82

Lodi Garden (p83) MUKUL BANERJEE/SHUTTERSTOCK ©

Top Sight 📷
Purana Qila

Shh, whisper it quietly: this place is better than the Red Fort. Delhi's 'Old Fort' isn't as magnificent in size and grandeur, but it's far more pleasant to explore, with tree-shaded landscaped gardens to relax in, crumbling ruins to climb over and no uptight guards with whistles telling you not to go here and there.

◎ MAP P82, E1

Old Fort

☎ 011-24353178

Mathura Rd

Indian/foreigner ₹25/300, with card ₹20/250, moat ₹20, video ₹25

🕐 dawn-dusk

Ⓜ Pragati Maidan

History

Purana Qila, or 'Old Fort', is what remains of the sixth of Delhi's eight historic cities, and dates from the 16th century. Ringed by a moat, part of which has been refilled with water, and accessed through the majestically imposing **Bada Darwaza** gateway, this fort is where Mughal Emperor Humayun met his end in 1556, tumbling down the steps of the octagonal **Sher Mandal**, which he used as a library.

The fort had originally been built by Afghan ruler Sher Shah (1538–45), during his brief ascendancy over Humayun.

Grounds

Groups of teenagers hang out with their friends, families picnic on the lawns and the more adventurous of visitors risk their lives, clambering up onto the crumbling outer walls. You could easily spend a couple of hours in here, exploring the ruins or just chilling out in the gardens.

Monuments

The fort's peaceful landscaped gardens are studded with well-preserved ancient red-stone monuments, including the intricately patterned **Qila-i-Kuhran Mosque** (Mosque of Sher Shah), behind which are tunnels to explore and outer walls that can be climbed upon. There's also a small **museum** (closed on Fridays) set within the walls just inside Bada Darwaza gateway. A **Sound & Light Show** (adult/child ₹100/50) is performed every evening beside the **Humayuni Darwaza** gateway, except on Fridays.

★ Top Tips

∘ An elongated lake has been created from the fort's former moat, and in late afternoon it's well worth wandering along as the sun lights up the towering walls above it, making for fabulous sunset photos. You'll have to buy an extra ₹20 'moat ticket' along with your main ticket in order to explore it.

∘ Across busy Mathura Road are more relics from the same era, including the beautiful **Khairul Manazil** (Mathura Rd; Ⓜ Pragati Maidan) mosque, still used by local Muslims and a favoured haunt of flocks of pigeons.

✕ Take a Break

The landscaped gardens inside the fort are perfect picnic territory, which is handy because there's nowhere to buy food or drink here. Don't forget to bring water with you.

Top Sight
Humayun's Tomb

Said to have been the inspiration for the design of the Taj Mahal, this stunning Mughal tomb pre-dates its more famous cousin by 60 years. Unlike the Taj it wasn't constructed entirely from white marble, but with a combination of marble and red sandstone. It lacks the delicate finesse of India's most famous monument, but it shares its sublime symmetrical elegance.

◉ MAP P82, F3

Mathura Rd

Indian/foreigner ₹40/600, with card payment ₹35/550, video ₹25

🕑 dawn-dusk

Ⓜ JLN Stadium, Hazrat Nizamuddin

Striking Architecture

The arched facade of the main tomb is inlaid with bands of white marble and red sandstone, and the building follows strict rules of Islamic geometry, with an emphasis on the number eight. Visitors can climb up onto its red sandstone-paved platform, and explore the top level of the tomb, before looking out over the beautifully landscaped gardens.

Landscaped Gardens

The surrounding gardens are a joy, and perfect picnic material. They also contain lots more impressive monuments; gateways, tombs and the tall, imposing walls which enclose the entire complex.

Other Features

To your right as you enter the complex, Isa Khan's beautiful **tomb** (included in Humayun's Tomb entry fee; ⏱dawn-dusk) is a handsome example of Lodi-era architecture, constructed in the 16th century. Look out too for **Arab-ki-Sarai**, a 15m-tall gateway that served as the southern entrance to Arab Sarai, an area built to accommodate the Persian craftsmen who built the tomb. Nearby is the plainer but no less grand **Bu-Halima** gateway.

As part of a huge ongoing restoration project, a new state-of-the-art visitor centre is being built just outside the entrance, and will have walkways linking the complex with neighbouring Sunder Nursery and Hazrat Nizam-ud-din Dargah across Mathura Rd.

★ Top Tips

It's worth incorporating a visit here with a visit to Sunder Nursery (p83), next door, and Hazrat Nizam-ud-din Dargah (p80), just across the main road. The new underground passageway, linking the three sites, will make access between the three much easier, and will form part of a modern tourist interpretation centre, when it eventually opens, that is. The original intended completion date was 2017!

✕ Take a Break

There's nowhere to eat at Humayun's Tomb, or in next door Sunder Nursery (though both locations are ideal for picnics), but there's plenty of street food and small restaurants in the narrow lanes outside Hazrat Nizam-ud-din Dargah, which is just across the main road, including a small branch of the famous Karim's (p86).

Top Sight 📷
Hazrat Nizam-ud-din Dargah

Visiting the marble shrine (dargah) of Muslim Sufi saint Nizam-ud-din Auliya is a unique experience, and one that will live long in the memory. It's an ancient site, but this is more than just a nod to Delhi's history; it's an opportunity to experience the magically spiritual atmosphere that emanates from the final resting place of this much-revered ascetic.

◎ MAP P82, E3

off Lodi Rd

🕐 24hr

Ⓜ JLN Stadium

Intensely Spiritual

Nizam-ud-din died in 1325 at the ripe old age of 92. His doctrine of tolerance made him popular not only with Muslims, but other faiths too, and devotees come in their hundreds each day to pay their respects, filling the shrine's surrounding courtyard with an intense spirituality that's rarely experienced outside festivals and special celebrations. The dargah is hidden away in a tangle of bazaars selling rose petals, attars (perfumes) and other offerings, and on some evenings you can hear Sufis singing *qawwali* (Islamic devotional singing), amid crowds of devotees.

In the central courtyard is an inlaid marble pavilion. Women are not supposed to go beyond the outer veranda, but they can peek through *jali* (lattice screens) to see the dark chamber where the grave of the great saint lies draped in robes and rose petals. Devotees tie threads to the *jali* for good luck.

Revered by Royals

Later kings and nobles wanted to be buried close to Nizam-ud-din, hence the huge number of Mughal tombs located in this part of the city, but there are also numerous other graves within the compound itself, including those of Jahanara (daughter of Shah Jahan) and the renowned Urdu poet Amir Khusru.

★ Top Tips

o You must remove your shoes before entering the shrine, but there's no need to do so whilst wandering the bazaars that approach it, despite pushy shoe-tenders telling you otherwise.

o When you leave, don't forget to give some money to whoever did look after your shoes; around ₹10.

o Entry is free, but you may be asked to make a donation.

o There's plenty to buy in the bazaars surrounding the shrine – great for unusual, inexpensive souvenirs like incense-stick holders, headscarves or prayer bells.

✗ Take a Break

Kebab stalls (p87) line the lanes here. For a proper meal, including standout goat curry, head to the small branch of Old Delhi's famous Karim's (p86), tucked away in one of the surrounding lanes; ask for directions.

Sunder Nagar, Nizamuddin & Lodi Colony

Ring Rd (MG Rd)

SUNDER NAGAR

Delhi Zoo
(National Zoological
Gardens)

Purana
Qila

Mathura Rd

NIZAMUDDIN
EAST

Sunder
Nursery

Bharat Scouts and
Guides Marg

Arab Ki
Sarai Marg

Humayun's
Tomb

Harsha Rd

Nizamuddin
Train Station

Khan-i-Khanan's
Tomb

Full Circle
Bookstore

Nizamuddin
Tomb

KAKA
NAGAR

Sher
Shah Rd

Dr Zakir Hussain Marg

Hazrat
Nizam-ud-din
Dargah

Lal Bahadur Shastri Marg

JANGPURA

Delhi
Golf
Course

Lodhi
Spa

Lodi Rd

NIZAMUDDIN
WEST

Jangpura

Pandara Rd

Khan
Market

PANDARA
PARK

Archbishop
Makarious Rd

Central Golf
Link Rd

JLN
Stadium

Barapullah
Elevated Rd

Garud Rd

Shah Jahan Rd

Humayun Rd

Maharishi Raman Marg

Khel Gaon Marg

See Enlargement

Tibet
House

Jor Bagh Rd

Sewa Nagar
Train Station

NEW
DELHI

Max Mueller Marg

Fourth Ave

Motilal
Nehru
Place

Subramania Bharti Rd

Prithviraj Rd

Sheesh Gumbad

Third Ave

The
Bookshop

Lodi Rd

LODI
COLONY

Second Ave

Aurangzeb Rd

Sikander Lodi's Tomb

Bada Gumbad

Lodi Garden

Mohammed
Shah's Tomb

JOR
BAGH

Lodi Colony
Train Station

MEENA
BAGH

Tees Jan Marg

Tughlaq Rd

Maulana Azad Rd

Krishna
Menon Marg

Udyog
Bhawan

Akbar Rd

Lok Kalyan
Marg

Nagaland
House

Tughlaq Rd

Aurobindo Marg

Safdarjang Rd

Safdarjang's
Tomb

Jor Bagh

Kamraj La

Rajaji Marg

Kamal Ataturk Rd

Golf
Course

Safdarjang
Aerodrome

DIPLOMATIC
ENCLAVE

Racecourse Rd

Panchsheel
Marg

Amatrra Spa

Gujarat
Bhawan

Nehru
Park

Racecourse

Sarojini Nagar
Train Station

Vinay Marg

Full Circle
Bookstore

Khan
Market

Anokhi

Fabindia

Kana

Bahrisons

Immigrant Cafe

Good Earth

0   100 m
0   0.05 miles

0   1 km
0   0.5 miles

Sights

Lodi Garden   PARK

1 ⊙ MAP P82, C3

Delhi's loveliest escape was originally named after the wife of the British Resident, Lady Willingdon, who had two villages cleared in 1936 in order to landscape a park containing the Lodi-era tombs. Today, these lush, tree-shaded gardens – a favoured getaway for Delhi's elite, local joggers and courting couples – help protect over 100 species of trees and 50 species of birds and butterflies, as well as half a dozen fabulously captivating 15th-century **Mughal monuments**. (Lodi Rd; ⏱6am-8pm Oct-Mar, 5am-8pm Apr-Sep; Ⓜ Khan Market, Jor Bagh)

Sunder Nursery   PARK

2 ⊙ MAP P82, E2

One of Delhi's newest tourist sights, this wonderful park was an overgrown wasteland until recent renovations brought the 16th-century Mughal gardens back to something approaching their former glory. It's now a vast landscaped heritage park with clipped lawns, delicate waterways and a network of paths dotted with fruit trees, flower beds, tree-shaded benches and numerous 16th-century **Mughal tombs** and **pavilions**, some of which still lie in a charming state of ruin, while some have been lovingly restored. (Mathura Rd; Indian/foreigner ₹35/100; ⏱dawn-dusk; Ⓜ Hazrat Nizamuddin, JLN Stadium)

Safdarjang's Tomb   MONUMENT

3 ⊙ MAP P82, B3

Built by the Nawab of Avadh for his father, Safdarjang, this grandiose, highly decorative mid-18th-century tomb, set within palm-lined gardens, is an example of late-Mughal architecture. There were insufficient

---

The Lodi Tombs

Wonderful Lodi Garden is not only a pleasantly green city-centre escape, it also houses some enchanting 15th-century Afghan-dynasty tombs which are scattered throughout the foliage.

The twin tombs of **Bada Gumbad** (Map p82, C3; ⏱6am-8pm Oct-Mar, 5am-8pm Apr-Sep; Ⓜ Khan Market, Jor Bagh) and **Sheesh Gumbad** (Map p82, C3; ⏱6am-8pm Oct-Mar, 5am-8pm Apr-Sep), both dating from 1494, the bulbous **Mohammed Shah's tomb** (Map p82, C3; ⏱6am-8pm Oct-Mar, 5am-8pm Apr-Sep), 1450, and the fortress-like walled complex of **Sikander Lodi's tomb** (Map p82, C2; ⏱6am-8pm Oct-Mar, 5am-8pm Apr-Sep), 1518, are the park's most notable structures, but also look for **Athpula**, an eight-piered bridge spanning a small lake, which dates from Emperor Akbar's reign.

funds for all-over marble, so materials to cover the dome were taken from the nearby mausoleum of Khan-i-Khanan, and it was finished in red sandstone. (Aurobindo Marg; Indian/foreigner ₹25/300, video ₹25; 🕐dawn-dusk; Ⓜ Jor Bagh)

National Rail Museum
MUSEUM

4 ◎ MAP P82, A4

A contender for one of Delhi's most enjoyable museums, the National Rail Museum has steam locos and carriages spread across 11 acres. Among the venerable bogies are the former Viceregal Dining Car, and the Maharaja of Mysore's rolling saloon.

The indoor gallery includes some great hands-on exhibits, a miniature railway, and two simulators (weekday/weekend ₹150/300). Outside, a toy train (weekday/weekend ₹100/200), a joy train (adult/child ₹20/10, weekend ₹50/20) and a steam train (₹200, Thursday and Saturday only) chuff around the grounds. (📞011-26881816; www.nr-mindia.com; Service Rd, Chanakyapuri; adult/child ₹50/10, Sat & Sun ₹100/20; 🕐10am-5pm Tue-Sun; Ⓜ Safdarjung)

Khan-i-Khanan's Tomb
HISTORIC BUILDING

5 ◎ MAP P82, F3

This is the monumental tomb of a poet and minister in Akbar's court. Khan-i-Khanan had it built for his wife in 1598, and was buried here

Sunder Nursery (p83)

AZHAR_KHAN/SHUTTERSTOCK ©

himself in 1627. It was later plundered to build nearby Safdarjang's tomb, and more of its decoration was stripped in the 19th century. (Rahim Khan Marg; Indian/foreigner ₹25/300, with card payment ₹20/250; ⏱dawn-dusk; Ⓜ Hazrat Nizamuddin)

Tibet House
MUSEUM

6 ◉ MAP P82, D3

Showing valuable Tibetan items brought out of Tibet following Chinese occupation, this forgotten-feeling small museum has a fine collection of jewel-like sacred manuscripts, votive carvings and around 200 historic *thangkas* (Tibetan cloth paintings). Photography is prohibited. (☎011-24603652; http://tibethouse.in; 1 Lodi Rd; ₹10; ⏱9.30am-5.30pm Mon-Fri; Ⓜ JLN Stadium)

Amatrra Spa
SPA

7 ◉ MAP P82, A2

Amatrra is where the A-list come to be pampered, with ayurvedic treatments and conventional massages starting at ₹2500 per hour. (☎011-24122921; www.amatrraspa. com; Ashok Hotel, Chanakyapuri; massage treatments ₹2500-7500; ⏱8am-8.30pm; Ⓜ Lok Kalyan Marg)

Lodhi Spa
SPA

8 ◉ MAP P82, E3

The fragrant, rarefied world of the Lodhi spa is open to nonguests who book treatments, such as massages, facials and traditional ayurvedic treatments. (☎011-43633333; www.thelodhi.com; Lodhi Hotel, Lodi Rd; 1hr massage from ₹3800; Ⓜ JLN Stadium)

Eating

Indian Accent
INDIAN $$$

9 🍴 MAP P82, E3

Inside luxury Lodhi hotel, though privately run, Indian Accent is one of the capital's top dining experiences. Chef Manish Mehrotra works his magic using seasonal ingredients married in surprising and beautifully creative combinations. The tasting menu is astoundingly good, with wow-factor combinations such as tandoori bacon prawns or paper dosa filled with wild mushroom and water chestnuts. Dress smart. Book ahead. (☎011-26925151; https://indianaccent. com/newdelhi; Lodhi Hotel, Lodi Rd; dishes ₹500-1750, tasting menu veg/nonveg ₹3600/3900; ⏱noon-2.30pm & 7-10.30pm; Ⓜ JLN Stadium)

Mamagoto
ASIAN $$$

10 🍴 MAP P82, A1

Fun, friendly and fabulously colourful, this laid-back east-Asian restaurant, with funky manga art and retro Chinese posters on the walls, has an eclectic menu spanning Japan, China and Southeast Asia – including noodles, dumplings and some authentically spicy hawker-style Thai food. (☎011-45166060; 53 Middle Lane, Khan Market; mains ₹400-800; ⏱12.30-11.30pm; Ⓜ Khan Market)

Sodabottleopenerwala

PARSI $$$

11 MAP P82, A1

The name is like a typical trade-based Parsi surname, the place emulates the Iranian cafes of Mumbai, and the food is authentic Persian, including vegetable berry pilau, mixed-berry trifle and *lagan nu custer* (Parsi wedding custard). (www.sodabottleopenerwala.in; Khan Market; mains ₹325-745; ⏰9am-midnight; Ⓜ Khan Market)

Perch

INTERNATIONAL $$$

12 MAP P82, A1

The coolification of upscale shopping enclave Khan Market continues apace with Perch, a wine bar–cafe that's all pared-down aesthetic, waiters in pencil-grey shirts, soothing music, international wines and pleasing international snacks such as Welsh rarebit and tiger prawn with soba noodles. (☎9728603540; Khan Market; dishes ₹325-975, wine per glass ₹325-800, cocktails ₹500-650; ⏰8am-midnight; 📶; Ⓜ Khan Market)

Karim's

MUGHLAI $$

13 MAP P82, E3

Hidden down the buzzing alleys that surround Hazrat Nizam-ud-din Dargah is this branch of historic Karim's, serving meaty Mughlai delights such as tasty

Cheap Embassy Bites

If you find yourself at a loose end in the diplomatic enclave, struggling to find anywhere affordable to eat, then make a beeline for Kautilya Marg. This road is lined with state bhavans, which act like Delhi consulates for the different states of India, and some of them open their staff canteens to the public for breakfast, lunch and dinner. The food is always cheap (you'll pay around ₹100 for a lunchtime thali), very filling (you usually get unlimited refills) and fabulously authentic (they tend only to use genuine, regionally sourced ingredients), and gives you the opportunity to try out different regional cuisines from across the country.

Gujarat Bhawan (Map p82, A2; 11 Kautilya Marg, Chanakyapuri; breakfast ₹60, thalis ₹110-140; ⏰7.30-10.30am, 12.30-3pm & 7.30-10pm; 📷; Ⓜ Lok Kalyan Marg) is a good choice at No 11, but there are also bhavans for Bihar, Tamil Nadu and Karnataka, among others. Further east from here is the unusual **Nagaland House** (Map p82, B2; 29 Dr APJ Abdul Kalam Rd; thalis ₹120-200; ⏰7-9am, noon-3pm & 7.30-10pm; Ⓜ Lok Kalyan Marg), a bhavan with especially friendly staff that serve pork specialities from the far-off north-eastern state of Nagaland.

National Rail Museum (p84)

kebabs and rich curries. (168/2 Jha House Basti; dishes ₹120-400; ☉1-3pm & 6.30-11pm Tue-Sat; Ⓜ JLN Stadium)

Altitude Cafe & Deli
CAFE $$$

14 Ⓧ MAP P82, D4

This fully organic cafe, with lots of gluten-free choices, has Turkish and Blue Tokai (Delhi's best, locally roasted) coffee, as well as great salads, burgers, pizzas, eggs Benedict and more, and you can take away jams, cakes and other snacks from the deli counter. (www.thealtitudecafe.com; 116 Meharchand Market; mains ₹340-580; ☉8.30am-7.30pm; 🛜; Ⓜ JLN Stadium)

Kebab Stands
STREET FOOD $

15 Ⓧ MAP P82, E3

The alleyways in front of Hazrat Nizam-ud-din Dargah are full of eateries all day long, but become a hive of activity every evening as devotees leave the shrine in search of sustenance. Canteen-style kebab houses cook up lip-smacking beef, mutton and chicken offerings at bargain prices, with biryani and roti as filling side orders. (Hazrat Nizam-ud-din Dargah; kebabs from ₹30; ☉noon-11pm; Ⓜ JLN Stadium)

Basil & Thyme
ITALIAN $$$

16 Ⓧ MAP P82, E2

This elegant icon buzzes with expats and well-to-do locals, who

Experiencing Khan Market

Though at first glance a bit rough around the edges, **Khan Market** (Map p82, A1; ⏱10.30am-8pm Mon-Sat; Ⓜ Khan Market) is in fact one of Delhi's most upmarket shopping enclaves. It's reported to be the most expensive place to rent a shop in India, and is favoured by moneyed middle-class locals and expats. Its boutiques focus on fashion, books and homewares, but it's also a great place to come for food and drink.

Book lovers should head to Full Circle Bookstore (p90) or Bahrisons (p90). For Indian clothing and homewares, try **Fabindia** (Map p82, A1; Khan Market; ⏱10.30am-9.30pm), **Anokhi** (Map p82, A1; www.anokhi.com; 32 Khan Market; ⏱10am-8pm), or **Good Earth** (Map p82, A1; 9 ABC Khan Market; ⏱11am-8pm), and for elegantly packaged *ayurvedic* remedies, try **Kama** (Map p82, A1; 22A Khan Market; ⏱10.30am-8.30pm).

Of the numerous cafes, Café Turtle is popular, though Big Chill buzzes with shoppers too, and has a spin-off bakery and ice-cream shop. Restaurants also abound; Upmarket Perch (p86) has a strong wine list; Sodabottleopenerwala (p86) is a funky Parsi-cuisine specialist; for Mexican, try **Immigrant Cafe** (Map p82, A1; ☏011-43105777; 29, 1st fl, Middle Lane, Khan Market; dishes ₹325-525; ⏱noon-midnight).

flock to dine on delicate Mediterranean flavours, in a quiet location in leafy Sundar Nagar. (☏011-24357722; www.basilandthyme.in; Sundar Nagar Market; mains ₹550-1200; ⏱noon-10pm; Ⓜ Khan Market)

Diva Spiced
ASIAN $$$

17 🍴 MAP P82, D3

The newest opening from chef Ritu Dalmia, this chic, airy eatery offers tapas-style and full-size Asian dishes, with tantalising, taste-tingling combinations such as prawn with mango and snow peas, as well as recommended burgers

like the soy and wasabi–infused chicken burger. (www.divarestaurants.com; 79-80 Meharchand Market, Lodi Colony; dishes ₹550-1350; ⏱11.30am-11.30pm; Ⓜ JLN Stadium)

Sagar Ratna
SOUTH INDIAN $$

Housed within the grandiose Ashok hotel (see 7 ◎ Map p82, A2), this branch of venerable South Indian restaurant Sagar Ratna is considered the best of all the locations around town. It's often buzzing with families and couples, and does a great line in dosas, *idlis* (spongy fermented rice cake), *uttapams* (savoury rice pancakes) and thalis. There are other branches in **Connaught Place** (15 K-Block, Connaught Place; dishes ₹110-285; 8am-11pm; M Rajiv Chowk) and **Defence Colony** (18 Block A, Defence Colony Market; dishes ₹150-250; 8am-11pm; M Lajpat Nagar). (The Ashok, 50B, Diplomatic Enclave; dishes ₹300-470, thali ₹530; 8am-11pm; M Lok Kalyan Marg)

Drinking

Big Chill
CAFE

18 MAP P82, A1

Popular, film-poster-lined cafe at Khan Market, packed with chattering Delhiites. The menu is a telephone directory of Continental and Indian dishes (₹290 to ₹625). Nearby is its spin-off

cakery (for cakes and pastries) and **creamery** (for ice cream). (Khan Market; noon-11.30pm; M Khan Market)

Café Turtle
CAFE

19 MAP P82, A1

Allied to the Full Circle Bookstore (p90), this brightly painted boho cafe gets busy with chattering bookish types, and is ideal when you're in the mood for coffee and cake in cosy surroundings, with a leafy outdoor terrace as well. There is also a **branch** (8 Nizamuddin East Market; dishes ₹375-545, coffees from ₹200; 8.30am-8.30pm; M Jangpura) in Nizamuddin East. (Khan Market; dishes ₹375-545; 8.30am-8.30pm; M Khan Market)

Khan Market

Bookworms Delight

There are bookshops all over Delhi, but this unassuming neighbourhood hides some gems. Khan Market houses two of them: the delightful **Bahrisons** (Map p82, A1; www.booksatbahri.com; Khan Market; ⏰10.30am-7.30pm Mon-Sat, 11am-7pm Sun; Ⓜ Khan Market) and the city's best branch of **Full Circle Bookstore** (Map p82, A1; www.fullcirclebooks.in; 23 Khan Market; ⏰8.30am-8.30pm).

In nearby Jor Bagh Market you'll find the much-loved **Bookshop** (Map p82, C3; 13/7 Jor Bagh Market; ⏰10.30am-7pm Mon-Sat; Ⓜ Jor Bagh), founded in 1970 by the late Kanwarjit Singh Dhingra, and a genteel institution amongst the bookworms of South Delhi.

Latitude 28°
CAFE

20 🍴 MAP P82, A1

Above the bijou Good Earth homewares store, this is Khan Market's prettiest cafe, awash with colour and sparkly chandeliers, with global snacks, such as plantain fried rice and sweet potato burgers with sour cream, plus teas, coffees and a strong wine list. (2nd fl, Good Earth, Khan Market; dishes ₹500-1000; ⏰11.30am-11pm; Ⓜ Khan Market)

Diggin Cafe
CAFE

Cute cafe with shaded terrace seating, serving pizza, pasta and salads in this serene garden shopping complex (see 24 🔒 Map p82, A2). (Santushti Shopping Complex, Kamal Ataturk Rd; dishes ₹400-500; ⏰11.30am-10.30pm; Ⓜ Lok Kalyan Marg)

Entertainment

Habitat World
LIVE PERFORMANCE

21 ⭐ MAP P82, D3

This is an important Delhi cultural address, with art exhibitions, performances and concerts, mostly free. Check the website for events. (☎011-43663333; www.habitatworld.com; India Habitat Centre, Lodi Rd; Ⓜ Jor Bagh)

India International Centre
LIVE PERFORMANCE

22 ⭐ MAP P82, C3

The IIC is a key location for a sector of Delhi society, usually elderly intellectuals. Although the club is for members only, the public is welcome to the regular, quality, free exhibitions, talks and concerts. (☎011-24619431; www.iicdelhi.nic.in; 40 Max Mueller Marg; Ⓜ Khan Market)

Shopping

Meharchand Market
MARKET

23 🔒 MAP P82, D3

Across the road from the government housing of the Lodi Colony, this is a long strip of small boutiques selling homewares and clothes. Quality clothing shops include **Play Clan** (☎011-24644393; www.theplayclan.com; shop 17-18, Lodi Rd; ⏱10.30am-7.30pm; 🚻) and **The Shop** (⏱10am-8pm Mon-Sat, 11am-7pm Sun), while stand-out eateries are the fully organic Altitude Cafe & Deli (p87), the Middle Eastern sweets and coffee shop **Kunafa** (sweets per kg from ₹300, coffee ₹250; ⏱10am-10pm), and Asian-tapas restaurant Diva Spiced (p88). (Lodi Colony; Ⓜ JLN Stadium)

Santushti Shopping Complex
MARKET

24 🔒 MAP P82, A2

Diplomats frequent this exclusive and serene shopping complex in which upmarket clothing,

jewellery and souvenir boutiques are housed inside little pavilions dotted around a garden. Stores include tea specialists **Aap Ki Pasand** (San Cha; ☎011-264530374; www.sanchatea.com; ⏱10am-7pm Mon-Sat), clothing shop **Anokhi** (www.anokhi.com; ⏱10am-7pm Mon-Sat) and the cute Diggin Cafe with coffee, light lunches and shaded terrace seating. (Kamal Ataturk Rd, Santushti Enclave; ⏱10am-9pm; Ⓜ Lok Kalyan Marg)

Sundar Nagar Market
ARTS & CRAFTS

25 🔒 MAP P82, E2

Genteel and sleepy Sundar Nagar is a collection of boutique shops set around a small park and specialises in Indian and Nepali handicrafts, replica 'antiques', jewellery and Indian teas. There's also a popular sweet and snack shop, and the much-loved Italian restaurant Basil & Thyme (p87). (Mathura Rd; ⏱10.30am-7.30pm Mon-Sat; Ⓜ Khan Market)

Top Sight 📷
Akshardham Temple

Such are the tourist crowds and tight security at this famous Hindu temple – Delhi's largest – that visiting it is more akin to a theme-park experience than a spiritually religious one, but the architecture of the main buildings, and the craftsmanship of the carvings is truly exceptional and well worth hopping on the metro to see.

📞 011-43442344

www.akshardham.com

National Hwy 24, Noida turning

temple free, exhibitions & water show ₹250

🕑 temple 9.30am-6.30pm Tue-Sun, exhibitions 9.30am-5pm

Breathtaking Architecture

Built by the Gujarati Hindu Swaminarayan Group in 2005, Akshardham Temple is but a spring chicken in India's temple pantheon, but it is breathtakingly lavish. Artisans used ancient techniques to carve the pale red sandstone into elaborate reliefs, including 20,000 deities, saints and mythical creatures that decorate the exterior of the buildings; note the elephants surrounding the outside of the main temple.

Inside the main building, the centrepiece is a 3m-high **gold statue of Bhagwan Shri Swaminarayan**, a Hindi yogi and an ascetic to whom the temple is dedicated. His statue is surrounded by more, fabulously intricate carvings – it's such a shame you're not allowed to take photos, given the quality of the craftsmanship. Cameras are just one of the many items you're not allowed to bring inside.

The rearmost alcove of the main temple contains the holy relics of Bhagwan Shri Swaminarayan; his footprints, hair and clothes.

Extra Activities

Within the temple grounds, there are a few 'exhibitions' on offer, for which you need to buy a ticket for. They are displayed in three large halls and include historical dioramas, a cinema screen and a **boat ride** through 10,000 years of Indian history, with animatronics telling stories from the life of Swaminarayan. There's also an illuminated **water show** (tickets ₹80) that's held just after sunset.

In the main temple, you can witness devotees performing morning and evening *aarti* (prayers), usually held at 10am and 6pm.

A moat-like pond, called **Narayan Sarovar**, surrounds the main temple. It is said to contain the waters of 151 of India's holy rivers and lakes.

★ Top Tips

○ Security is exceptionally tight. All bags, large or small, and any possessions apart from your passport and wallet, must be deposited in the free bag-drop by the entrance. It's secure, but you might want to leave precious valuables like laptops or expensive cameras at your hotel.

○ It's free to get into the temple, but the 'exhibitions' ticket, which includes the boat ride, costs ₹250.

✕ Take a Break

You can't bring food or drinks into the complex, but there's an outdoor **food hall** within the temple compound where you can buy cheap set-meals, snacks and drinks.

★ Getting There

Ⓜ The temple is in the eastern suburbs, but just 200m walk from Akshardham metro station; turn right out of the station and take the first right.

Explore ◈

South Delhi

The quiet, leafy, largely affluent neighbourhood of South Delhi is where many expats and middle-class Delhiites choose to make their homes. For tourists, it makes a nice escape from the mayhem of the city centre, with most visitors focusing their attentions on the boutique shops, cafes and restaurants of Hauz Khas or Shahpur Jat Village.

The Short List

○ *Hauz Khas (p99)* Shopping and exploring the atmospheric ruins overlooking the 13th-century reservoir.

○ *Shahpur Jat Village (p105)* Eating and shopping your way around this arty, urban village, surrounded by the remains of Siri Fort's ancient walls.

○ *Wellness Treatments (p101)* Pampering yourself with an ayurvedic massage, or a meditation or yoga class, at one of the wellness centres, such as Kerala Ayurveda, near Hauz Khas.

○ *Saffron Palate (p100)* Learning how to master home-cooked Indian recipes.

○ *Bahai House of Worship (p99)* Marvelling at the Sydney Opera House–like architecture of this striking temple.

Getting There & Around

Ⓜ Most places are well served, though both Hauz Khas and Shahpur Jat Village are 1km from their nearest station.

Autorickshaws Ubiquitous. Along with e-rickshaws, they form a scrum outside metro stations, looking for passengers.

Cycle-rickshaws Less common out here, but still service the residential estates.

Neighbourhood Map on p98

Bahai House of Worship (p99) designed by architect Fariborz Sahba
SAIKO3P/SHUTTERSTOCK ©

Walking Tour 🥾

Haus Kauz

Like a quaint little village in the suburbs of a mega city, Hauz Khas has something for everyone: Hipsters hangout in its buzzy drinking spots; fashionistas browse the clothing boutiques; parents bring their kids to the deer park; and courting couples sit arm-in-arm on the ruins of Feroz Shah's 14th-century madrasa, looking out dreamily across the tree-lined waters of the ancient reservoir.

Walk Facts

Start Rose Garden;
Ⓜ IIT

End Hauz Khas Social;
Ⓜ Green Park

Length 2km; two to three hours

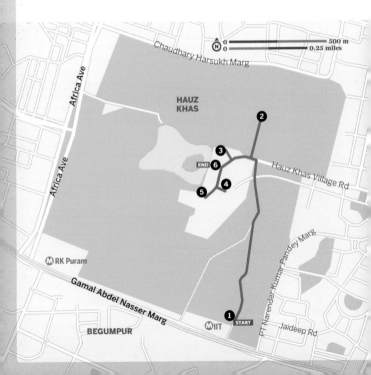

❶ Rose Garden

This peaceful, leafy, public park, 100m from IIT metro station, contains flower beds, outdoor exercise machines and even one or two roaming peacocks. It's a popular local hangout and its pathways lead all the way to Hauz Khas; keep walking north for about 1km and you'll eventually hit Hauz Khas Village Rd.

❷ Deer Park

The shops and cafes are all to your left, but for now walk straight on into the family-friendly **deer park** (Hauz Khas; admission free; ☉5am-8pm, to 7pm winter; Ⓜ IIT, Green Park). Its tree-shaded grounds offer cool respite from the heat, making it popular with local joggers too, but kids love the duck pond, the rabbit enclosures and, of course, the deer.

❸ All Arts

Come back the way you came, and turn right towards the cluster of boutique shops. Fancy, independent clothing stores abound, but for something a bit different, seek out All Arts (p105), a small basement arts shop, piled high with unusual Indian knick-knacks such as retro Bollywood cinema posters, old-school comics and Raj-era cigarette tins.

❹ Kunzum Travel Cafe

Back on the main drag, continue along Hauz Khas Village Rd, but turn left just before the main ruins, and look for the super-chilled Kunzum Travel Cafe (p104) on your right. There are no prices – you pay what you want as you leave – and you can browse travel books, get online and even get creative with the free-to-use paint sets.

❺ Feroz Shah's Madrasa

Left out of the cafe, and left again, brings you to Hauz Khas's historic highlight; the peaceful ruins of Feroz Shah's madrasa (p99). The ruins can be explored, but most people just perch on their favourite piece of 14th-century rubble and look out over the picturesque reservoir, surrounded by the forests of the neighbouring deer park.

❻ Hauz Khas Social

Head back to the main drag to end your stroll at buzzing Hauz Khas Social (p103), a cafe-restaurant-bar with gourmet burgers, craft beers and views over the ancient reservoir through floor-to-ceiling windows.

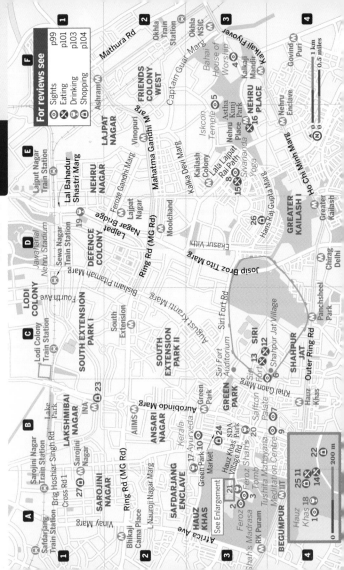

For reviews see

◎ Sights	p99
✕ Eating	p101
♦ Drinking	p103
⯃ Shopping	p104

Sights

Hauz Khas
AREA

1 ⊙ MAP P98, A4

Built by Sultan Ala-ud-din Khilji in the 13th century, Hauz Khas means 'noble tank', and its reservoir once covered 28 hectares. It collected enough water during the monsoon to last Siri Fort throughout the dry season. Today it's much smaller, but still a beautiful place to be, thronged by birds and surrounded by parkland. Overlooking it are the impressive ruins of Feroz Shah's 14th-century madrasa (religious school) and tomb, which he had built before his death in 1388. (⊙dawn-dusk; Ⓜ IIT)

Feroz Shah's Madrasa
RUINS

2 ⊙ MAP P98, A3

The impressive ruins of Feroz Shah's 14th-century madrasa overlook the tree-lined waters of Hauz Khas, and can be explored. You can climb down from here to the lake. To reach the ruins, walk to the end of the Hauz Khas shops, and you'll see the entranceway beside No 50. (Ⓜ IIT, Green Park, Hauz Khas)

Feroz Shah's Tomb
HISTORIC BUILDING

3 ⊙ MAP P98, A3

This small, beautiful tomb is the link between the two wings of Feroz Shah's madrasa. It's constructed from quartzite rubble and the fine decorative work is incised and painted plaster. The drum bears the 99 names of Allah. (Ⓜ Green Park, IIT)

Bahai House of Worship
TEMPLE

4 ⊙ MAP P98, F3

Designed for tranquil worship, Delhi's beautiful Lotus Temple offers a rare pocket of calm in the hectic city. This architectural masterpiece was designed by Iranian-Canadian architect Fariborz Sahba in 1986. It is shaped like a lotus flower, with 27 delicate-looking white-marble petals. The temple was created to bring faiths together; visitors are invited to pray or meditate silently according to their own beliefs. The attached visitor centre tells the story of the Bahai faith. Photography is prohibited inside the temple. (Lotus Temple; ☏011-26444029; www.bahaihouseofworship.in; Kalkaji; ⊙9am-7pm Tue-Sun Apr-Sep, to 5.30pm Oct-Mar; Ⓜ Okhla NSIC, Kalkaji Mandir, Nehru Place)

Iskcon Temple
TEMPLE

5 ⊙ MAP P98, F3

Close to the Bahai House of Worship, this flamboyant red and white temple opened in 1998, and is operated by the Hare Krishna movement. From Nehru Place metro station, you can walk through Astha Kunj Park to reach the temple (10-minute walk). (www.iskcondelhi.com; ⊙4.30am-1pm & 4-9pm; Ⓜ Nehru Place)

The Bahai Faith

The Bahai Faith which runs South Delhi's **Bahai House of Worship** (aka the Lotus Temple; p99) is one of the youngest, and most inclusive world religions. It was founded in 1863 in Iran by Bahá'u'lláh, who Bahais believe to be the most recent manifestation of God.

Unusually, the Bahai faith accepts all religions as having true and valid origins, and believes that people should work together for the common benefit of humanity. There is thought to be around six million Bahais in the world, including some 1.8 million in India, making this the largest Bahai community in the world.

Bahá'u'lláh recommended that Bahais should meditate for a period each day, thinking about what they have done during the day and what their actions are worth. The stunning Lotus Temple on the western fringes of South Delhi, was completed in 1986, and was built as a centre for meditation. Today, visitors of all faiths are invited to join Bahais for periods of silent, contemplative, meditation.

Siri Fort

FORT

6 ◉ MAP P98, C4

Only some of the walls remain of this 14th-century fort, built by Ala-ud-din Khilji as the second of the seven historical cities of Delhi. They are impressive nonetheless, and it is said that the heads of 8000 Mongols were buried into the foundations! Within the boundaries of the walls is an auditorium, a sports complex and the village of Shahpur Jat (p105), which contains an interesting collection of boutique shops and cafes hidden amongst its tight network of alleyways. (Ⓜ Hauz Khas, Green Park)

Saffron Palate

COOKING

7 ◉ MAP P98, B4

These award-winning Indian cookery classes are run by Neha Gupta in her family home and last for around three hours. The classes, which tend to start at 11am, culminate in a full-course Indian lunch. (☏ 9971389993; www.saffronpalate. com; R21 Hauz Khas Enclave; per person ₹4000; Ⓜ Hauz Khas)

Sivananda Yoga

HEALTH & WELLBEING

8 ◉ MAP P98, E3

This excellent ashram offers courses and workshops for both beginners and the advanced, plus drop-in classes ranging from one to two hours. On Sunday (12.30pm to 2pm) there is a free introductory drop-in class. (☏ 011-40591221; www.sivananda.org.in; A41 Kailash Colony; 3-week beginner course ₹4000; ⏱ 6am-8pm Mon-Fri, 8am-12.30pm Sat, 8am-2.30pm & 5.30-7.30pm Sun; Ⓜ Kailash Colony)

Tushita Mahayana Meditation Centre

MEDITATION

9 MAP P98, B4

Twice-weekly, guided, Buddhist meditation sessions in a peaceful, temple-like meditation hall. Sessions are free. Donations are welcomed. (☏011-26513400; http://tushitadelhi.com; 9 Padmini Enclave; admission free; ☻6.30-7.30pm Mon & Thu; Ⓜ Hauz Khas)

Kerala Ayurveda

AYURVEDA

10 MAP P98, B3

Treatments from *sarvang ksheerdhara* (massage with buttermilk) to *sirodhara* (warm oil poured on the forehead). (☏011-41754888; www.ayurvedancr.com; E-2 Green Park Extension, Green Park

Market; 1hr full-body massage from ₹1700; ☻8am-6.30pm; Ⓜ Green Park)

Eating

Naivedyam

SOUTH INDIAN $$

11 ✗ MAP P98, A4

This superb South Indian restaurant feels like a temple, with a woodcarved interior, waiters dressed as devotees, and incense burning on the exterior shrine. Diners receive a complimentary lentil soup-drink and pappadam as they browse the menu, which includes delectable dosas and to-die-for thalis. (☏011-26960426; dishes ₹150-200, thalis ₹275-380; ☻11am-11pm; Ⓜ Green Park)

Hauz Khas (p99)

HEMIS/ALAMY STOCK PHOTO ©

Dilli Haat (p104)

Potbelly

NORTH INDIAN $$

12 MAP P98, C3

It's a rare treat to find a Bihari restaurant in Delhi, and this artsy, shabby-chic place with fabulous views from its 4th-floor perch has authentic Bihari thalis and dishes such as *litti* chicken – whole-wheat balls stuffed with *sattu* (ground pulse) and served with *khada masala* chicken. (116C Shahpur Jat Village; dishes ₹150-450, thalis from ₹300; ⏰12.30-11pm; MHauz Khas, Green Park)

Cafe Red

CAFE $$

13 MAP P98, C3

A fun and trendy ground-floor cafe that's hidden down an alley and serves omelettes, sandwiches,

soups and pizza as well as espresso coffee and shakes. Has some patio seating, too. (5-G Jungi House, Shahpur Jat Village, Siri Fort; mains ₹150-300; ⏰10.30am-8.30pm; 📶 MHauz Khas, Green Park)

Coast

SOUTH INDIAN $$$

14 MAP P98, A4

A light, bright restaurant on several levels, with views over the parklands of Hauz Khas, chic Coast serves light South Indian dishes, such as *avial* (vegetable curry) with *risheri* (pumpkin with black lentils), plus tacos, burgers, salads and hit-the-spot mustard-tossed fries. Decent wine list, too. (📞011-41601717; Hauz Khas; dishes ₹360-580; ⏰noon-midnight; MGreen Park)

Evergreen
CAFE $

Part cafe, part sweet shop, Evergreen, located in Green Park Market (see 24 Map p98, B3) has been keeping punters happy since 1963 with its veg snacks, *chaat,* thalis and dosas. (S29-30 Green Park Market; dishes ₹100-200, thalis ₹165-240; ⏱9am-9pm; Ⓜ Green Park)

Big Chill Cafe
ITALIAN $$

15 Ⓧ MAP P98, E3

Very popular cafe-restaurant serving decent pizza, pasta and salads, plus good coffee and great shakes. Also serves alcohol. It opens out onto the pleasant horseshoe-shaped Kailash Colony Market, which has numerous cafes, restaurants and shops. (☎011-46556828; HS-5, Kailash Colony Rd, Sector 4, Kailash Colony Market; dishes from ₹300; ⏱noon-11.30pm; 📶; Ⓜ Kailash Colony)

Epicuria
FOOD HALL $$

16 Ⓧ MAP P98, E3

Part of the Nehru Place metro station complex, this popular basement-level food court has a variety of outlets, including Karim's (for kebabs) and Sagar Ratna (for South Indian), plus plenty more besides. You buy a card for ₹100, ₹200, ₹500 or ₹1000 then pay with it at any outlet – if there's change you can get the money back afterwards. (Nehru Place; meals from ₹150; ⏱11am-11pm; Ⓜ Nehru Place)

Drinking

Piano Man Jazz Club
CLUB

17 Ⓟ MAP P98, B3

The real thing, this popular, atmospheric place with proper musos is a dim-lit speakeasy with some excellent live jazz performances. (http://thepianoman.in; B-6 Commercial Complex, Safdarjung Enclave; ⏱noon-3pm & 7.30pm-12.30am; Ⓜ Green Park)

Hauz Khas Social
BAR

18 Ⓟ MAP P98, A4

This chilled-out restaurant-bar-club is a Hauz Khas hub, and has an urban warehouse-like interior with stone walls, high ceilings and huge plate-glass windows overlooking lush greenery and the Hauz Khas lake. There's an extensive

Siri Fort Auditorium

Built within the ruined grounds of the 14th-century Siri Fort (p100), this **venue** (Map p98, C3; https://in.bookmyshow.com; Aug Kranti Marg, Siri Fort Institutional Area, Siri Fort; Ⓜ Green Park) is one of Delhi's premier auditoriums and the headquarters of the Directorate of Film Festivals. The main auditorium has a capacity of 700 and is a great place to take in a concert, a play or a film screening. Check the website for schedules.

food menu (dishes ₹200 to ₹500) plus beers, cocktails and regular live music and DJs in the evenings. (www.socialoffline.in/HauzKhasSocial; 12 Hauz Khas Village; ⊙11am-12.30am; MGreen Park)

Ek Bar   BAR

19 🚇 MAP P98, D1

On the upper floors of a building in the exclusive area of the Defence Colony, this place has stylish, kooky decor in deep, earth-jewel colours, serious mixology (cocktails from ₹475) showcasing Indian flavours (how about a gin and tonic with turmeric?), modern Indian bar snacks, nightly DJs, and a see-and-be-seen crowd. (D17, 1st fl, Defence Colony; ⊙5pm-1am; MLajpat Nagar)

Summer House Cafe   BAR

20 🚇 MAP P98, B3

Close to Hauz Khas, this roomy, rustic 1st-floor bar has a spacious terrace and is a popular, lively evening haunt for a mixed crowd of men and women. There's frequent live music or DJs (from 9pm), a wide-ranging multicuisine menu serving everything from fish and chips to Thai curries, and a Kingfisher costs ₹195. (1st fl, Aurobindo Place Market; dishes ₹400-600, beers from ₹160; ⊙noon-1am; MGreen Park)

Kunzum Travel Cafe   CAFE

21 🚇 MAP P98, A3

Quirky Kunzum has a pay-what-you-like policy for the French-

press coffee and tea, and sells its own brand of travel guides to Delhi. There's free wi-fi, a few travel books and magazines to browse, and paints and brushes on a table for you to produce your own artwork. (www.kunzum.com; T49 Hauz Khas Village; ⊙11am-7.30pm Tue-Sun; 🛜; MGreen Park)

Shopping

Hauz Khas
Village   HANDICRAFTS, CLOTHING

22 🔒 MAP P98, B4

This arty little enclave has narrow lanes crammed with boutiques selling designer Indian clothing, handicrafts, contemporary ceramics, handmade furniture and old Bollywood posters. Intriguingly, it's located beside numerous 13th- and 14th-century ruins (p99), as well as a forested deer park (p97) and a lake. Standout eating and drinking options include Naivedyam (p101) and Hauz Khas Social (p103). (Hauz Khas Fort Rd; ⊙11am-7pm Mon-Sat; MIIT)

Dilli Haat   ARTS & CRAFTS

23 🔒 MAP P98, B1

Right beside INA metro station, this popular, but somewhat stage-managed, open-air food-and-crafts market is a cavalcade of colour and sells regional handicrafts from all over India; bargain hard. At the far end are food stands where you can sample cuisine from every corner of the country. Beware impostors; this

Shahpur Jat Village

Located within the boundaries of the ruined walls of Siri Fort (p100), **Shahpur Jat Village** (Map p98, C4; ◷10am-7pm Mon-Sat; Ⓜ Hauz Khas, Green Park) contains an artsy collection of high-end clothing boutiques, health-conscious cafes and no-frills eateries, many of which are hidden amongst a network of graffiti-splattered alleyways, making this one of Delhi's more intriguing places to shop.

Standout shops include **Aum** (www.aumdelhi.com; 5G Jungi House, Shahpur Jat Village, Siri Fort; ◷11am-7pm Mon-Sat), for fabulously colourful contemporary Indian women's clothing, and **NeedleDust** (www.needledust.com; 40B, ground fl, Shahpur Jat; ◷10.30am-7.30pm Mon-Sat), for exquisite embroidered jooti (leather slippers). For food, try the excellent, affordable Bihari restaurant Potbelly (p102), or hip, yet laidback Cafe Red (p102).

is the only real Dilli Haat in Delhi. (Aurobindo Marg; Indian/foreigner ₹30/100; ◷10.30am-10pm Mar-Nov, 11am-9pm Dec-Feb; Ⓜ INA)

Fabindia
CLOTHING

24 🔒 MAP P98, B3

Branch of the excellent Indian clothing shop, with a wide range of men's cotton kurtas (long shirts) and pyjamas, women's *salwar kameez* (dress-like tunic and trouser combinations) and a few well-designed homewares. (S-37, Green Park Market; ◷10.30am-8.30pm; Ⓜ Green Park)

All Arts
ART

25 🔒 MAP P98, A4

An Aladdin's Cave of unusual Indian-retro arty souvenirs, including Bollywood cinema posters, prints of old Delhi maps, cigarette tins and old India postcards. It's to your right as you enter the village,

round the back of Naivedyam restaurant. (1 Hauz Khas Village; ◷11am-8pm; Ⓜ IIT)

M-Block Market
MARKET

26 🔒 MAP P98, D3

This pleasant collection of clothing boutiques, jewellery shops, cafes, ice-cream parlours and restaurants, strung out along a quiet, tree-shaded avenue, attracts middle-class shoppers and expats. (M-Block, Greater Kailash; ◷10am-8pm Wed-Mon; Ⓜ Kailash Colony)

Sarojini Nagar Market
CLOTHING

27 🔒 MAP P98, A1

Beside the metro station of the same name, this frenetic flea market is the place to come for cut-price clothes, with minor faults or blemishes. (Sarojini Nagar; ◷10am-9pm Tue-Sun; Ⓜ Sarojini Nagar)

Explore ◎
Greater Delhi & Gurgaon (Gurugram)

This vast neighbourhood includes some of Delhi's standout archaeological sites – Qutab Minar, Mehrauli, Tughlaqabad – but venture further out, to the village–turned–cyber city of Gurgaon, and you'll witness an incredible contrast. Here, super-slick sky trains carry you above the gnarly traffic as they zip their way between shopping malls, hotels, restaurants and bars – welcome to the Delhi of the future!

The Short List

○ **Qutab Minar (p109)** *Craning your neck as you gaze upwards in awe at the remarkable 73m-tall, 900-year-old Afghan-style victory tower.*

○ **Mehrauli Archaeological Park (p110)** *Wandering the fabulous scattered ruins of this little-visited park.*

○ **Tughlaqabad (p114)** *Exploring the fascinating remains of the still-mighty bastions of this sprawling 14th-century fort.*

○ **Kingdom of Dreams (p118)** *Whooping, cheering and whistling your way through a Bollywood-style theatre extravaganza; Gurgaon's best show.*

Getting There & Around

Ⓜ The Delhi Metro links this neighbourhood to the centre, while Gurgaon's sky train, Rapid Metro, zips shoppers around.

Autorickshaws You'll often have to take an auto or e-rickshaw the last few kilometres from your destination station.

Neighbourhood Map on p112

Qutab Minar (p109) EMAD ALJUMAH/GETTY IMAGES ©

Top Sight 📷
Qutab Minar Complex

Centred on its astonishing namesake tower, the Qutab Minar Complex is arguably Delhi's stand-out historical sight, and despite its distance from the city centre shouldn't be missed by any first-time visitor to the capital. The park-like grounds are enjoyable to stroll around – this is great picnic territory – and the ruins themselves, though not vast, are fascinating to explore.

◉ MAP P112, E1

📞 011-26643856

Indian/foreigner ₹40/600, with card payment ₹35/550

🕓 dawn-dusk

Ⓜ Qutab Minar

History

Some of the ruins here are remnants of Delhi's first incarnation, the ancient city of Lal Kot, which was established around AD 736, though the site's most striking remains were added later on. The first monuments were erected by the sultans of Mehrauli, and subsequent rulers expanded on their work, hiring the finest craftsmen and artisans to set in stone the triumph of Muslim rule.

Qutab Minar

The site is dotted with ruined tombs and monuments, but the glorious highlight is the unmissable, soaring Afghan-style **Qutab Minar**, the victory tower and minaret, erected by sultan Qutb-ud-din in 1193 to proclaim his supremacy over the vanquished Hindu rulers of Qila Rai Pithora. Ringed by intricately carved sandstone bands bearing verses from the Quran, the tower stands nearly 73m tall and tapers from a 15m-diameter base to a mere 2.5m at the top.

Quwwat-ul-Islam Masjid & Iron Pillar

At the foot of the Qutab Minar stands **Quwwat-ul-Islam Masjid** (Might of Islam Mosque), the first mosque to be built in India, and Delhi's main mosque until 1360. As well as intricate carvings that show a clear fusion of Islamic and pre-Islamic styles, the walls of the mosque are studded with sun disks, shikharas (rising towers) and other recognisable pieces of Hindu and Jain masonry. The exquisite marble and sandstone **Alai Darwaza gatehouse** was added to it in 1310.

Close by is a 6.7m-high **iron pillar**, thought to be 1600 years old. It hasn't rusted in that time due to both the dry atmosphere and its incredible purity.

★ **Top Tips**

o There are eateries outside the entrance, but there's nowhere to buy food or drink inside, so be sure to bring plenty of water and snacks if you plan on staying a while.

o For safety reasons, tourists can no longer climb the tower, but there are incredible photo opportunities of the ruins, even from ground level – late afternoon has the best light, but crowds are thinner first thing in the morning.

✗ **Take a Break**

Exit the complex and turn left to find a bunch of places to eat and drink, including snack stalls, a branch of **Cafe Coffee Day** and various fast-food outlets.

For somewhere nicer, follow the main road round to the back of the complex where there's a cluster of high-end restaurants, including the lovely Mediterranean courtyard restaurant, Olive (p117).

Top Sight 📷

Mehrauli Archaeological Park

Even if it wasn't for the astonishing collection of ruins scattered around Mehrauli, this would be a lovely forested park in which to stretch your legs after a visit to nearby Qutab Minar; wild pigs and troops of monkeys scamper about, while bright-green parakeets flit from tree to tree.

◉ MAP P112, E2

admission free

🕑 dawn-dusk

Ⓜ Qutab Minar

Mehrauli Monuments

Aside from the green spaces, the park also happens to contain more than 400 ancient monuments, dating from the 10th century right up to the British era, making it an unmissable destination for anyone with even a passing interest in the history of Delhi.

Most impressive are the time-ravaged **tombs** of Balban and Quli Khan, his son, and the **Jamali Khamali mosque** (pictured), attached to the tomb of the Sufi poet Jamali. To the west is the 16th-century **Rajon ki Baoli**, Delhi's finest step-well, with a monumental flight of steps leading down to what is, these days, a small pool of water, and one which is often completely dry.

Northern Section

At the northern end of Mehrauli village, which lies just beyond the park, is **Adham Khan's Mausoleum**, which was once used as a British residence, then later as a police station and post office. Leading northwards from the tomb are the pre-Islamic **walls of Lal Kot**, Delhi's first city.

Southern Section

To the south of the village are the remains of the Mughal palace, the **Zafar Mahal**, once in the heart of the jungle. Next door to it is the Sufi shrine, the **Dargah of Qutab Sahib**. There is a small burial ground with one empty space that was intended for the last king of Delhi, Bahadur Shah Zafar, who died in exile in Burma (Myanmar) in 1862. South of here is a Lodi-era burial ground for *hijras* (transvestites and eunuchs), Hijron ka Khanqah (p113). The identity of those buried here is unknown, but it's a well-kept, peaceful place, revered by Delhi's *hijra* community. A little further south are **Jahaz Mahal** ('ship palace', also built by the Mughals) and the Haus i Shamsi tank (p113).

(p113)

★ **Top Tips**

○ Despite being a forest of sorts, the tree cover is sparse and the terrain often dry and dusty, making for uncomfortable walking in the midday heat. Try to visit in the early morning if possible, before continuing on to Qutab Minar afterwards.

○ Mehrauli is perfect picnic territory, but do beware of marauding monkeys, at their most active, it seems, in the cooler late afternoon.

○ It's easy to get lost in the park, so stick to the footpaths, some of which have signposts pointing out the better-known sights.

✗ **Take a Break**

Bringing a picnic is a good idea, but you'll find cheap local restaurants beyond the park in **Mehrauli village**. There are more eating options outside the entrance to nearby Qutab Minar.

Greater Delhi & Gurgaon (Gurugram)

For reviews see

Chirag Delhi
Outer Ring Rd
MALVIYA NAGAR
Jahanpanah Forest
Lal Bahadur Shastri Marg
Mehrauli Badarpur Rd
Aurobindo Marg
Malviya Nagar
Press Enclave Marg
SAKET
Saket
Champa Gali
Qutab Minar Complex
Westend Marg
Garden of the 5 Senses
BEGUMPUR
Alai Minar
MEHRAULI
Qutab Minar
Mehrauli Archaeological Park
Hijron ka Khanqah
Hauz i Shamsi Tank
Chhatarpur
Chhatarpur Mandir
Jawaharlal Nehru University
Nelson Mandela Rd
Aruna Asaf Ali Marg
Mehrauli Rd
Sultanpur
Aurobindo Marg
Ghitorni
Sanskriti Museums
Arjan Garh
Mandi Rd
Gurgaon Rd
Gurgaon Rd
Cyber City
DLF Cyber Hub
Guru Dronacharya
Sikanderpur
MG Road
IFFCO Chowk
Delhi-Gurgaon Expressway
Faridabad-Gurgaon Rd
Phase 1
Golf Course Rd
HUDA City Centre

2 km
1 mile

Sights

Champa Gali ARTS CENTRE

1 ⦿ MAP P112, E2

The small arty enclave known as Champa Gali is hidden away in the lanes behind the fake Dilli Haat handicrafts market ('Delhi Haat') and is one of Greater Delhi's best-kept secrets. It's a favourite for Delhi's fashionistas, and contains a cluster of craft boutiques and cool cafes, including standout coffee roasters Blue Tokai (p117) and tea specialists Jugmug Thela (p118). It's tough to find; turn left out of Saket metro station, take the first left, then turn left down Lane 3. You'll reach the open courtyard on your right, through an inconspicuous gateway with no sign. (Lane 3, West End Marg, Saket; Ⓜ Saket)

Hijron ka Khanqah ISLAMIC SITE

2 ⦿ MAP P112, D2

At this seemingly long-forgotten yet immaculately maintained site, 49 *hijras* are buried in simple white tombs. The more elaborate grave, chequered in green and white, is that of the sister of a man known as Sheikh Baba. The site is tricky to find, but is reached by a grill-covered doorway on the street north of Jahaz Mahal. (Kalka das Marg; ⊙ dawn–dusk; Ⓜ Qutab Minar)

Sanskriti Museums MUSEUM

3 ⦿ MAP P112, C3

On the way to Gurgaon, this little-known, well-kept place contains museums devoted to 'everyday art' and Indian terracotta and textiles. Much of the museum is outside and covers 7 acres. Objects such as kitchenware and hookahs are works of art, and there are expressive terracotta sculptures and intricate textiles from Gujarat, Rajasthan, Kashmir and Bengal. The complex is about 1km walk north of Arjan Garh metro station; follow the main road northeast, then turn left. (www.sanskritifoundation.org/museums.htm; Anandagram, Mehrauli Gurgaon Rd; free; ⊙ 10am–5pm Tue–Sun; Ⓜ Arjan Garh)

Haus i Shamsi Tank MONUMENT

4 ⦿ MAP P112, D2

This 12th-century reservoir was formerly larger. The pavilion at its edge was once in the middle, and supposed to cover the hoofprint of a horse, ridden by the Prophet, who appeared to Iltutmish of the Slave Dynasty in a dream and instructed him where to build the tank. The **Jahaz Mahal**, a 15th-century palace, overlooks it. (off Mehrauli-Gurgaon Rd; Ⓜ Qutab Minar)

Chhatarpur Mandir HINDU TEMPLE

5 ⦿ MAP P112, E2

Delhi's second-largest temple (after Akshardham), this impressive sandstone and marble complex dates from 1974, and is dedicated to the goddess Katyayani (one of the nine forms of Parvati). There are dozens of shrines with towering South Indian *gopurams* (temple towers), and an enormous statue of Hanuman stands guard

The Ruined Fortress of Tughlaqabad

This magnificent 14th-century ruined **fort** (Indian/foreigner ₹30/300, with card payment ₹25/250; ◷dawn-dusk; Ⓜ Govind Puri), half reclaimed by jungle and gradually being encroached on by villages, was Delhi's third incarnation, built by Ghiyas-ud-din Tughlaq. The sultan poached workers from the Sufi saint Nizam-ud-din, who issued a curse that shepherds would inhabit the fort. However, it is monkeys rather than shepherds that have since taken over. There are fantastic emerald-green views to be had from on top of the fort's mighty ramparts, and intriguing interlinking underground rooms can be explored.

The sultan's well-maintained sandstone **mausoleum** once stood in the middle of a lake, but now is separated from his fallen city by a road. It's included in the entry ticket. The ruins of the fort are fairly deserted, so it's best to visit them in a group; you could easily spend a couple of hours exploring. It does get hot out here, so bring plenty of water and snacks – there's nowhere to buy anything.

To reach the fort, take a private autorickshaw (around ₹50) from the Govind Puri metro station. Shared autos (₹10) from the metro station tend only to take you to the end of Guru Ravi Das Marg, leaving you to walk the final 500m to the entrance.

over one part of the complex, which is split by the road leading from the metro station. The smaller temples opposite the Hanuman statue actually have more of a spiritual buzz. (Shri Adya Katyayani Shakti Peeth Mandir; ☏ 011-26802360; www.chhattarpurmandir.org; Main Chhatarpur Rd; ◷4am-midnight; Ⓜ Chhatarpur)

Jahanpanah Forest
PARK

6 ◉ MAP P112, F1

Jahanpanah means 'refuge of the world', and is the fourth city of Delhi, founded in the 14th century by Muhammed Tughlaq, who thought his father's city at Tughlaqabad was unliveable. This 435-hectare, forested site has a dusty running track and a few scant ruins, including **Satpula bridge**. The forest is generally dry and dusty, but is well shaded, and bougainvillea and peacocks add splashes of colour. (Ⓜ Greater Kailash, Chirag Delhi)

Alai Minar
TOWER

7 ◉ MAP P112, E1

In the 14th century, Sultan Ala-ud-din made additions to the Qutab Minar Complex (p108), which included an ambitious plan to erect a second tower of victory, twice as high as Qutab Minar. Construction got as far as the first level before the sultan died; none of his successors saw fit to bankroll this extravagant piece of showboating. The 27m-high plinth can be seen just north of the Qutab Minar. Admission price is to the whole Qutab Minar Complex. (Indian/foreigner ₹40/600, with card payment ₹35/550; M Qutab Minar)

Garden of the 5 Senses
PARK

8 👁 MAP P112, E2

For a restful stroll, these landscaped gardens are filled with intriguing contemporary sculptures, wind chimes and lily ponds, and are popular with couples. To get here turn left out of Saket metro station, then left down Westend Marg. (📞 011-29536401; Westend Marg, off Mehrauli-Badarpur Rd; ₹35; 🕘 9am-6pm Oct-Mar, to 7pm Apr-Sep; M Saket)

Eating

Madhuban
ANDHRA $

9 ✖ MAP P112, A4

This very popular no-frills place serves authentic Andhra-style sattvik food, a yogic dietary tradition based on pure and energy-rich foodstuffs. *Pesarattu* (₹195), a popular breakfast staple, is a fabulous way to start the day when paired with the industrial strength filter coffee (₹75). Madhuban is one of a number of good eateries at Cross Point Mall, about 1.5km from IFFCO Chowk metro station; walk south, then take the first big left. (📞 0124-4300714; www.madhubanfoods.com; 2nd fl, Cross Point Mall, DLF City Phase IV, Gurugram; dishes from ₹100; 🕘 8am-10.45pm; P ❄ 🍴 👪; M IFFCO Chowk)

Garden of the 5 Senses

RAVINDERKANYAL/SHUTTERSTOCK ©

Cyber Hub Social   MULTICUISINE $$

Not quite as popular as its Hauz Khas sister, this branch of Social in DLF Cyber Hub (see 16 ⭐ Map p112, A3) is funky nonetheless, with a faux old-city terrace, including washing hanging beside your table, and private 'rooms' inside giant industrial concrete pipes. Good for a beer as well as a bite to eat. Menu covers Indian, pizza, burgers and more. (DLF Cyber Hub; dishes ₹200-500; ⏱11am-11pm; Ⓜ Cyber City)

Kheer   INDIAN $$$

10 ❌ MAP P112, C1

Upscale Indian restaurant housed in an atmospheric hotel, Kheer welcomes with its cheery decor reminiscent of warm Kashmiri households. Aside from quality delicacies, expect a *chaat* (snack)

bar serving scrumptious street-food in fine surrounds. A mixology bar adds to the special experience. (📞011-71558800; www.roseate hotels.com; Roseate House New Delhi, Asset 10, Hospitality District, Aerocity; mains ₹1000-3000; ⏱7.30-11pm; Ⓟ❄️📶🚻; Ⓜ Aerocity)

Rose Cafe   CAFE $$$

11 ❌ MAP P112, E2

Opposite the fake Dilli Haat market, 'Delhi Haat', an unprepossessing building harbours the Rose Cafe, prettily pale blue and pink. It's all cake stands and freshly prepared Mediterranean and comfort food, with heart-warming dishes such as shepherd's pie, pancakes and all-day breakfasts. (📞011-29533186; 2 Westend Marg, Saidullajab; dishes ₹300-600; ⏱noon-9pm; Ⓜ Saket)

Select Citywalk (p119)

Food Court Dining 🍽

DLF Cyber Hub (Map p112, A3; www.dlfcyberhub.com; DLF Cyber City, Phase II, NH-8; ⊙most restaurants 11am-11pm, bars to 1am; Ⓜ Cyber City) is a food court par excellence. You'll find any type of cuisine you fancy, from Indian street food and Tibetan *momos* (dumplings) to high-end European and chic cafe bites. Tables spill out onto the large plaza; there's also an indoor 1st-floor food court with some cheaper options.

Standouts include **Burma Burma** (☏0124-4372997; www.burmaburma.in; dishes ₹300-500; ⊙noon-3pm & 7-11pm), for Southeast Asian food; the cool Cyber Hub Social, with funky terrace seating and private rooms; **Farzi Cafe** (www.farzicafe.com; dishes ₹400-600; ⊙11am-1am), for upmarket Indian street food; People & Co (p119) for live comedy; **Yum Yum Cha** (dim sum from ₹345, sushi from ₹485; ⊙12.30-11pm) for dim sum and sushi; and Soi 7 (p118) for craft beer brewed on-site. For a cheaper, on-the-hop option, grab a filter coffee (₹35) from the teeny stairwell takeaway **Madras Coffee House**.

Olive
MEDITERRANEAN $$$

12 ⊗ MAP P112, E1

There are plenty of cafes and fast-food joints near the entrance to Qutab Minar, but if you fancy eating in style after visiting the ruins, follow the road around the back of the complex to beautiful Olive, with its *haveli* courtyard setting and award-winning Mediterranean menu. (☏011-29574443; Bhulbhulaiya Rd, behind Qutab Minar, Mehrauli; pizza from ₹950, meze platters from ₹1500; ⊙noon-midnight; Ⓜ Qutab Minar)

Diva
ITALIAN $$$

13 ⊗ MAP P112, F1

Delhi uberchef Ritu Dalmia's flagship is this *molto chic* Italian restaurant with its light-filled space on two levels, starched tablecloths, plate-glass windows, and sophisticated modern Italian cuisine, such as slow-cooked pork with raspberry jus, as well as crispy wood-fired pizzas. (☏011-29215673; M8, M-Block market, Greater Kailash II; mains ₹600-1600; ⊙12.30-4pm & 7pm-midnight; Ⓜ Greater Kailash)

Drinking

Blue Tokai
CAFE

Found in a magically unexpected art enclave called Champa Gali (see 1 ◉ Map p112, E2), Blue Tokai is one of a few cool cafes here – but it's the one the coffee aficionados come to. It grinds its own beans here and you can get serious caffeine hits such as nitrogen-infused cold brew. (www.bluetokaicoffee.com; Champa Gali, Lane 3, West End Marg, Saket; coffee from ₹100, snacks ₹150-300; ⊙9am-10pm; 🛜; Ⓜ Saket)

Jugmug Thela TEAHOUSE

Another hidden surprise in Champa Gali (see 1 ◉ Map p112, E2) – the mini art enclave down Lane 3 behind the fake Dilli Haat store – this tea specialist has more than 180 herbs and spices to work with. It serves delicious ayurvedic teas and other blends, plus organic coffee and fabulously unique sandwich combos (spicy potato and pomegranate; almond and banana) that shouldn't work, but do. (www.jugmugthela.com; Champa Gali, Lane 3, Westend Marg, Saket; teas & coffees ₹70-100, sandwiches ₹120-280; ⏱10.30am-8.30pm; 🛜; Ⓜ Saket)

Soi 7 BAR

Up on the top floor of DLF Cyber Hub (see 16 ☆ Map p112, A3), this popular bar brews four different beers in-house (₹325 for a half-litre glass), stocks numerous single-malt whiskeys and whips up a range of cocktails. It does food, too. (DLF Cyber Hub; draught beer from ₹325; ⏱11am-1am; Ⓜ Cyber City)

Entertainment

Kingdom of Dreams THEATRE

14 ☆ MAP P112, A4

An entertainment extravaganza, Kingdom of Dreams offers live Bollywood-style shows that are out-and-out sensory assaults. Performances are supported by world-class techno-wizardry, as the cast swing, swoop and sing from the rafters. There's a free shuttle from the metro every 15 minutes, but it's only a 500m walk; come out of Gate 2 and take the first right. (📞0124-4528000; www.kingdomofdreams.in; Auditorium Complex, Sector 29, Gurgaon; shows Tue-Fri ₹1200-3200, Sat & Sun ₹1300-4200, refundable entry to Culture Gully ₹600; ⏱12.30pm-midnight Tue-Fri, noon-midnight Sat & Sun, showtimes vary; Ⓜ IFFCO Chowk)

Sulabh International Museum of Toilets

More than half of India's 1.3 billion people still don't have a toilet in their homes, but since 1970 the Sulabh NGO has worked to address India's sanitation issues, constructing new public toilets. The organisation also educates, and this quirky **museum** (📞011-25031518; www.sulabhtoiletmuseum.org; Sulabh Bhawan, Mahavir Enclave, Palam Dabri Marg; admission free; ⏱8am-8pm Mon-Sat, 10am-5pm Sun; Ⓜ Dashrathpuri) traces the history of the water closet from 2500 BC to modern times. It's 650m south of Dashrathpuri metro station, straight along the main road.

Open-Air Theatre

TRADITIONAL MUSIC

15 ⭐ MAP P112, A4

Next door to the extravagant, more well-known Kingdom of Dreams, this modest open-air theatre puts on free traditional-music performances every Saturday evening at 7.30pm. It's 400m from IFFC Chowk metro station; come out of Gate 2 and take the first right. (admission free; ⊙7.30pm Sat; Ⓜ IFFCO Chowk)

People & Co

COMEDY

16 ⭐ MAP P112, A3

A restaurant and bar with comedy nights every evening, usually from around 7.30pm. Some nights are free. Bigger names bring a cover charge (from ₹500). Check the website for listings. (www.canvaslaughclub.com; DLF Cyber Hub; ⊙nightly; Ⓜ Cyber City)

Shopping

Select Citywalk

MALL

17 🅰 MAP P112, F1

Enormous, supermodern shopping complex containing three or four interconnected shopping malls, a handful of five-star hotels and even an art gallery. The central mall – Select Citywalk – has top-end clothing stores, plus restaurants, cafes and a couple of cinemas. Attached DLF Place contains more of the same, while the stylish **Kiran Nadar Museum**

of Art (☏011-49160000; www.knma.in; 145 DLF South Court Mall, Select Citywalk, Saket; admission free; ⊙10.30am-6.30pm Tue-Sun) is housed in the DLF South Court. (www.selectcitywalk.com; Press Enclave Marg, Saket; ⊙10am-11pm; Ⓜ Malviya Nagar)

Atelier Mon

FASHION & ACCESSORIES

18 🅰 MAP P112, B4

Mother-daughter team Monica Sharma and Meher Sra produce jewellery from naturally shaped semi-precious stones encased in precious metal. Come for a pocket-friendly array of rings, chunky bracelets, earrings, chains and signature neckpieces studded with agates, garnets, turquoise, pearls, lapis lazuli and coral. (www.ateliermon.com; 27/4, Deodar Marg, Block A, Sector 26A, opposite Qutab Plaza; ⊙11am-6pm Mon-Sat; Ⓜ Phase 1)

Kama Ayurveda

COSMETICS

19 🅰 MAP P112, A4

Kama specialises in premium-quality skin-, hair- and body-care products in beautiful packaging, all made using traditional ayurvedic ingredients. It's one of a number of shops and eateries in the pleasant and popular outdoor Galleria Market, about 1km from IFFCO Chowk metro station; walk south then take the first big left. (www.kamaayurveda.com; shop 32, Galleria Market, Gurgaon; ⊙11am-10pm; Ⓜ IFFCO Chowk)

Explore ◈

Agra

The magical allure of the Taj Mahal draws tourists to Agra like moths to a wondrous flame. And despite the hype, it's every bit as good as you've heard. But the Taj is not a standalone attraction. The legacy of the Mughal empire has left a magnificent fort and a liberal sprinkling of fascinating tombs and mausoleums. The busy bazaars are great fun too.

The Short List

○ **Taj Mahal (p122)** *Basking in the beauty of India's most iconic building.*

○ **Agra Fort (p126)** *Wandering the many rooms of one of India's most impressive ancient forts.*

○ **Mehtab Bagh (p130)** *Relaxing in gardens with perfect sunset views of the Taj.*

○ **Itimad-ud-Daulah (p134)** *Marvelling at the marble-work of an exquisite tomb nicknamed the Baby Taj.*

○ **Akbar's Mausoleum (p131)** *Visiting the impressive resting place of the greatest Mughal emperor.*

Getting There & Around

🚆 Express trains are well set up for day trippers to/from Delhi, but trains run between the two cities all day.

🚖 There's a pre-paid taxi rank outside Agra Cantonment train station.

Autorickshaw Once in Agra, you'll be zipping around in these most of the time.

Cycle-rickshaw For shorter, cheaper, more leisurely trips.

Neighbourhood Map on p128

Taj Mahal (p122) SCOTT BIALES/SHUTTERSTOCK ©

Top Sight 📸
Taj Mahal

Rudyard Kipling described it as 'the embodiment of all things pure', while its creator, Emperor Shah Jahan, said it made 'the sun and the moon shed tears from their eyes'. Every year, eight million tourists come to catch a once-in-a-lifetime glimpse of what is widely considered the most beautiful building in the world. Few leave disappointed.

◎ **MAP P128, G3**

☎ 0562-2330498

www.tajmahal.gov.in

Indian/foreigner ₹50/1100, mausoleum ₹200, video ₹25

🕐 dawn-dusk Sat-Thu

A Brief History

The Taj was built by Shah Jahan as a memorial for his third wife, Mumtaz Mahal, who died giving birth to their 14th child in 1631. The death of Mumtaz left the emperor so heartbroken that his hair is said to have turned grey virtually overnight. Construction of the Taj began the following year; although the main building is thought to have been built in eight years, the whole complex was not completed until 1653. Not long after it was finished, Shah Jahan was overthrown by his son Aurangzeb and imprisoned in Agra Fort, where for the rest of his days he could only gaze out at his creation through a window. Following his death in 1666, Shah Jahan was buried here alongside his beloved Mumtaz.

In total, some 20,000 people from India and Central Asia worked on the building. Specialists were brought in from as far away as Europe to produce the exquisite marble screens and pietra dura (marble inlay work) made with thousands of semiprecious stones.

The Taj was designated a World Heritage Site in 1983 and looks nearly as immaculate today as when it was first constructed – though it underwent a huge restoration project in the early 20th century.

Inside the Grounds

From both the east and west gates you first enter a monumental inner courtyard with an impressive 30m red-sandstone **gateway** on the south side.

The **ornamental gardens** are set out along classical Mughal *charbagh* (formal Persian garden) lines – a square quartered by watercourses, with an ornamental marble plinth at its centre. When the fountains are not flowing, the Taj is beautifully reflected in the water.

On the western side of the gardens, is the small but excellent **Taj Museum** (admission

★ Top Tips

∘ Help the environment by entering the mausoleum barefoot instead of accepting the free disposable shoe covers.

∘ Bring a small torch into the mausoleum to fully appreciate the translucency of the white marble and semi-precious stones.

✗ Take a Break

You can't take food inside the grounds, and none is available to buy either, but there are numerous places to eat a stone's throw away in Taj Ganj.

free; ⏱10am-5pm Sat-Thu), housing a number of original Mughal miniature paintings, including a pair of 17th-century ivory portraits of Emperor Shah Jahan and his beloved wife Mumtaz Mahal. It's well worth visiting before you leave.

The Mausoleum

The Taj Mahal itself stands on a raised marble platform at the northern end of the ornamental gardens, with its back to the Yamuna River. Its raised position means that the backdrop is only sky – a masterstroke of design. Purely decorative 40m-high white **minarets** grace each corner of the platform. After more than three centuries they are not quite perpendicular, but they may have been designed to lean slightly outwards so that in the event of an earthquake they would fall away from the precious Taj. The red-sandstone **mosque** (pictured p122) to the west is an important gathering place for Agra's Muslims. The identical building to the east, the **Jawab**, was built for symmetry.

The central Taj structure is made of semitranslucent white marble, carved with flowers and inlaid with thousands of semiprecious stones in beautiful patterns. A perfect exercise in symmetry, the four identical faces of the Taj feature impressive vaulted arches embellished with pietra dura scrollwork and quotations from the Quran in a style of calligraphy using inlaid jasper. The whole structure is topped off by four small domes surrounding the famous bulbous central dome.

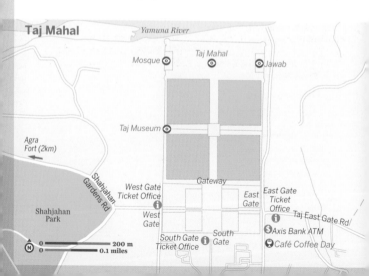

Need to Know

o The Taj is closed every Friday to anyone not attending prayers at the mosque.

o Your basic entry ticket only gets you into the grounds of the Taj; a further ticket is needed to enter the mausoleum itself.

o Cameras and videos are permitted, but you can't take photographs inside the mausoleum. Tripods are banned.

o The Taj can be accessed through the west and east gates. The south gate was closed to visitors in 2018 for security concerns but can be used to exit the Taj.

o Remember to retrieve your free 500ml bottle of water (included in Taj ticket price), but skip the environmentally unsound, disposable shoe covers.

o Bags much bigger than a money pouch are not allowed inside; free bag storage is available. Any food or tobacco will be confiscated when you go through security, as will pens.

Directly below the main dome is the **Cenotaph of Mumtaz Mahal**, an elaborate false tomb surrounded by an exquisite perforated marble screen inlaid with dozens of different types of semiprecious stones. Beside it, offsetting the symmetry of the Taj, is the **Cenotaph of Shah Jahan**, who was interred here with little ceremony by his usurping son Aurangzeb in 1666. Light is admitted into the central chamber by finely cut marble screens.

The real tombs of Mumtaz Mahal and Shah Jahan are in a basement room below the main chamber.

Top Sight 📷
Agra Fort

With the Taj Mahal overshadowing it, one can easily forget that Agra has one of the finest Mughal forts in India. Walking through courtyard after courtyard of this palatial red-sandstone and marble fortress, your amazement grows as the scale of what was built here begins to sink in. Distant views of the Taj are an added bonus.

◎ MAP P128, C2

Lal Qila

Indian/foreigner ₹50/650, video ₹25

⊙dawn-dusk

A Colossal Entrance

The fort was built in 1565 by Emperor Akbar and its colossal, 2.5km-long double walls rise more than 20m up. The Yamuna River originally flowed along its eastern edge. **Amar Singh Gate** is the sole entry point these days. Its dog-leg design was meant to confuse attackers.

You soon reach the huge red-sandstone **Jehangir's Palace** on the right, while further along the eastern edge you'll find the **Khas Mahal**, a beautiful marble pavilion and pool that formed the living quarters of Shah Jahan. Taj views are framed cutely in the ornate marble grills.

Shah Jahan's Prison

Just to the north of the Khas Mahal is **Mathamman (Shah) Burj**, a wonderful white-marble octagonal tower and palace where Shah Jahan was imprisoned for eight years until his death in 1666, and from where he could gaze out at the Taj Mahal, the tomb of his wife.

The Legendary Peacock Throne

Further along the eastern wall is **Diwan-i-Khas** (Hall of Private Audiences), which was reserved for important dignitaries. It once housed Shah Jahan's legendary Peacock Throne, which was in-set with precious stones – including the famous Koh-i-noor Diamond. The throne was taken to Delhi by Aurangzeb, then to Iran by Nadir Shah and dismantled after his assassination in 1747.

Ladies of the Court

Further north, a side door off a courtyard leads to the tiny but exquisite white-marbled **Nagina Masjid** (Gem Mosque; pictured), built in 1635 by Shah Jahan for the ladies of the court.

A hidden doorway near the mosque exit leads down to the scallop-shaped arches of the **Diwan-i-Am** (Hall of Public Audiences), which features a beautifully decorated throne room.

★ Top Tips

○ You can walk to the fort from the Taj, via the leafy Shah Jahan Park, or take an auto-rickshaw for ₹80.

○ The fort opens 30 minutes before sunrise; the ticket office opens 15 minutes before that. Last entry is 30 minutes before sunset.

✕ Take a Break

Food is not allowed into the fort (though you can bring water), and there are no decent restaurants nearby, so try to plan your visit between mealtimes.

Agra

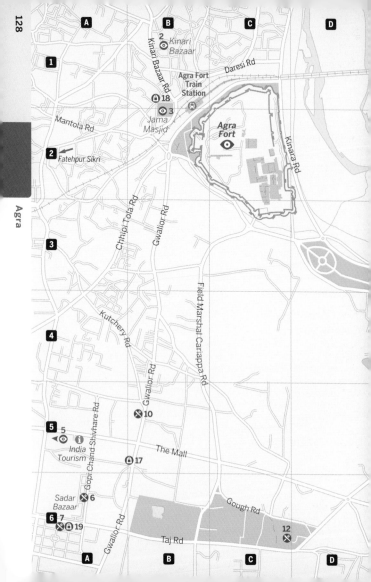

A

B

C

D

1

Kinari Bazaar Rd

2 Kinari Bazaar

Daresi Rd

Agra Fort Train Station

18

3

Jama Masjid

Mantola Rd

Agra Fort

2 Fatehpur Sikri

Kinara Rd

Chhipi Tola Rd

Gwalior Rd

3

Field Marshal Cariappa Rd

Kutchery Rd

4

Gwalior Rd

10

5 5

India Tourism

The Mall

17

Gopi Chand Shivhare Rd

Sadar Bazaar 6

Gough Rd

6 7

19

12

Gwalior Rd

Taj Rd

A

B

C

D

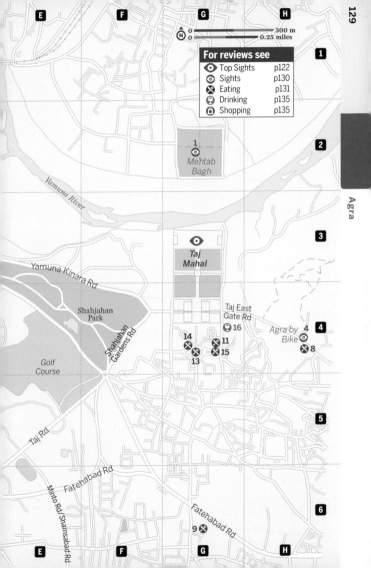

For reviews see
◉	Top Sights	p122
◎	Sights	p130
✖	Eating	p131
🍷	Drinking	p135
🛍	Shopping	p135

N 0 ——— 500 m
0 ——— 0.25 miles

Yamuna River

1 ◎ Mehtab Bagh

◉ Taj Mahal

Yamuna Kinara Rd

Shahjahan Park

Shahjahan Gardens Rd

Golf Course

Taj East Gate Rd
🍷 16

14 ✖
13 ✖
11 ✖
15 ✖

Agra by Bike ◎ 4
✖ 8

Taj Rd

Fatehabad Rd

Minto Rd/Shamsabad Rd

Fatehabad Rd

9 ✖

Sights

Mehtab Bagh PARK

1 ◎ MAP P128, G2

This park, originally built by Emperor Babur as the last in a series of 11 parks on the Yamuna's east bank (long before the Taj was conceived), fell into disrepair until it was little more than a huge mound of sand. To protect the Taj from the erosive effects of the sand blown across the river, the park was reconstructed and is now one of the best places from which to view the great mausoleum. (Indian/foreigner ₹25/300, video ₹25; ⊙dawn-dusk)

Kinari Bazaar MARKET

2 ◎ MAP P128, B1

The narrow streets behind Jama Masjid are a crazy maze of overcrowded lanes bursting with colourful markets. There are a number of different bazaars here, each specialising in different wares, but the area is generally known as Kinari Bazaar as many of the lanes fan out from Kinari Bazaar Rd. You'll find clothing, shoes, fabrics, jewellery, spices, marblework, snack stalls and what seems like 20 million other people. (⊙11am-9pm Wed-Mon)

Jama Masjid MOSQUE

3 ◎ MAP P128, B2

This fine mosque, built in the Kinari Bazaar by Shah Jahan's daughter in 1648 and once connected to Agra Fort, features striking zigzag marble patterning on its domes. The entrance is on the east side. (Jama Masjid Rd; ⊙dawn-dusk)

Touring Agra

Many folks spend but a day in Agra, taking in the Taj and Agra Fort and sailing off into the sunset. If you're interested in digging a little deeper, **Agra Walks** (☏9027711144; www.agrawalks.com; ₹2500) offers excellent walking/cycle-rickshaw combo tours that will show you sides of the city most tourists don't see. Old Agra highlights include going deeper into Kinari Bazaar and a few off-the-beaten-path temples such as Mankameshwar Mandir and Radha Krishna Mandir. A delectable food tour takes in five stops and includes tastings.

If you can't be bothered handling the logistics, look no further than **Amin Tours** (☏9837411144; www.daytourtajmahal.com) for all-inclusive private Agra day trips from Delhi by car (from US$85 per person, depending on number in group) or express train (from US$90 per person). Caveat: if they try to take you shopping and you're not interested, politely decline.

Akbar's Mausoleum

This outstanding sandstone and marble **tomb** (Indian/foreigner ₹30/310, video ₹25; ⊙dawn-dusk) commemorates the greatest of the Mughal emperors. The huge courtyard is entered through a stunning gateway decorated with three-storey minarets at each corner and built of red sandstone strikingly inlaid with white-, yellow- and blue-marble geometric and floral patterns. The interior vestibule of the tomb is stunningly decorated with painted alabaster, creating a contrast to the plain inner tomb. The unusual upper pavilions are closed. Look for deer in the surrounding gardens.

The mausoleum is at Sikandra, 10km northwest of Agra Fort. Catch a bus (₹25, 45 minutes) headed to Mathura from **Bijli Ghar** (Agra Fort Bus Stand; ☑0562-2464557) bus stand; they go past the mausoleum. Or else take an autorickshaw (₹350 return) or an Ola taxi.

Agra by Bike
CYCLING

4 ⊙ MAP P128, H4

John and Moses Rosario get rave reviews for their bike tours of the city and surrounding countryside, most of which end with a boat trip on the Yamuna River behind the Taj. They also offer food walks and Indian cooking classes. (☑9368112527; www.agrabybike.com; East Gate Rd; per person US$30)

UP Tourism
BUS

5 ⊙ MAP P128, A5

UP Tourism runs coach tours that leave Agra Cantonment train station at 10.30am Saturday to Thursday, after picking up passengers arriving from Delhi on the Taj Express. The whistle-stop tour includes the Taj Mahal, Agra Fort and Fatehpur Sikri, with a scant 1¼-hour stop in each place. (☑0562-2421204; www.uptourism. gov.in; incl entry fees Indian/foreigner ₹750/3600; ⊙9am-5pm Mon-Sat)

Eating

Mama Chicken
DHABA $$

6 ⊗ MAP P128, A6

This superstar *dhaba* (casual eatery) is a must: duelling veg and nonveg glorified street stalls employ 24 cooks during the rush, each of whom handles outdoor tandoors, grills or pots. They whip up outrageously good 'franky' rolls (like a flatbread wrap) – including a buttery-soft chicken tikka variety – along with excellent chicken curries, superb naan breads and evening-only chicken tandoori *momos* (Tibetan dumplings). (Stall No 2, Sadar Bazaar; rolls ₹40-190, mains ₹230-290; ⊙noon-midnight)

IGOR DYMOV/SHUTTERSTOCK ©

Mehtab Bagh (p130)

Agra Chat House
STREET FOOD $

7 MAP P128, A6

This classic *chaat* (snack) house is the oldest of a dozen street stalls just off Sadar Bazaar. Choose several dishes such as the *aloo tikki chat* (fried potato croquettes with tamarind sauce, yoghurt, coriander and pomegranate), *dahi bada* (dumplings with yoghurt and tamarind), *galgapa/pani puri* (puri shells filled with flavoured sauce), and eat them while standing with other appreciative diners. (Chaat Galli, Sadar Bazaar; snacks ₹50-60; 1-11pm)

Esphahan
NORTH INDIAN $$$

8 MAP P128, H4

There are only two sittings each evening at Agra's finest restaurant, so booking ahead is essential, especially as non-hotel-guest tables are limited. The exquisite menu is chock-full of unique delicacies, with the modern fusion tasting menus and Indian thalis offering the best selection. (0562-2231515; Taj East Gate Rd, Oberoi Amarvilas Hotel; mains ₹1550-3500; dinner 6.30pm & 9pm;)

Pinch of Spice
MODERN INDIAN $$$

9 MAP P128, G6

This modern North Indian superstar is the best spot outside five-star hotels to indulge yourself in rich curries and succulent tandoori kebabs. The *murg boti masala* (chicken tikka swimming in a rich and spicy gravy) and the *paneer lababdar* (unfermented cheese cubes in a spicy red gravy with sauteed onions) are outstanding. There's also a full bar. (www.pinchofspice.in; 1076/2 Fatehabad Rd; mains ₹375-450; ⏱noon-11.30pm)

Dasaprakash SOUTH INDIAN $$

10 🍴 MAP P128, B5

Fabulously tasty and religiously clean, Dasaprakash whips up consistently great South Indian vegetarian food, including spectacular thalis, *dosas*, a *rasum* (South Indian soup with a tamarind base) of the day and a few token Continental dishes. The ice-cream desserts are another speciality. Comfortable booth seating and wood-lattice screens make for intimate dining. (www.dasaprakashgroup.com; Meher Cinema Complex, Gwailor Rd; mains ₹210-360; ⏱noon-10.45pm; ❄🖊)

Saniya Palace Hotel MULTICUISINE $

11 🍴 MAP P128, G4

With cute tablecloths, dozens of potted plants and a bamboo pergola for shade, this is the most pleasant rooftop restaurant in Taj Ganj. It also has the best rooftop view of the Taj, bar none. The kitchen is a bit rough and ready, but the Western dishes and Western-friendly Indian dishes are fine and you are really here for the views. (Chowk Kagziyan, Taj South Gate; mains ₹100-200; ⏱6am-10pm; 📶)

Mughal Room NORTH INDIAN $$$

12 🍴 MAP P128, C6

The best of three eating options at Clarks Shiraz Hotel, this top-floor restaurant serves up sumptuous Mughlai and regional cuisine. Come for a predinner drink (beer ₹400) at the Sunset Bar for distant views of the Taj and Agra Fort. There's live Indian classical music here every evening at 8.30pm. Book a window table. (54 Taj Rd; mains ₹900-1500; ⏱7.30-11pm Mon-Fri, 12.30-3pm & 7.30-11pm Sat & Sun)

Snack Alley's Street Food 🍽

Fans of street food should make a beeline for Sadar Bazaar district, where you can fill up in *chaat galli* (snack alley), home to a dozen excellent street-food stalls.

First port of call is Agra Chat House, the oldest of the street stalls, or the next-door Agarwal Chat House, to invest in a selection of *aloo tikki chaat* (fried potato croquettes with tamarind sauce, yoghurt, coriander and pomegranate), *dahi bada* (dumplings with yoghurt and tamarind), *chila mong dal* (lentil pancake) or *galgapa* (little puri shells filled with flavoured sauce). At around ₹50 a dish you can afford to explore the simple menus.

Shankara Vegis   VEGETARIAN $

13 🍴 MAP P128, G4

Most restaurants in Taj Ganj ooze a distinct air of mediocrity – Shankara Vegis is different. This cosy old-timer, with its red tablecloths and straw-lined walls, stands out for great vegetarian thalis (₹140 to ₹250) and, most pleasantly, the genuinely friendly, nonpushy ethos of its hands-on owners. Try the rooftop. (Chowk Kagziyan; mains ₹90-150; ☉8am-10.30pm; 📶)

Joney's Place   MULTICUISINE $

14 🍴 MAP P128, G4

This pocket-sized institution whipped up its first creamy lassi in 1978 and continues to please despite cooking its meals in what must be Agra's smallest kitchen. The cheese and tomato 'jayfelles' (toasted sandwich), the banana lassi (with money-back guarantee) and the *malai* kofta (paneer cooked in a creamy sauce of cashews and tomato) all come recommended, but it's more about crack-of-dawn sustenance than culinary dazzle. (Kutta Park, Taj Ganj; mains ₹70-120; ☉5am-10.30pm)

Yash Cafe   MULTICUISINE $$

15 🍴 MAP P128, G4

This chilled-out, 1st-floor cafe has wicker chairs, sports channels on TV, DVDs shown in the evening and a good range of meals, from good-value set breakfasts to thalis (₹90), pizza (₹90 to ₹300) and Indian-style French toast (with coconut – we think

---

The Baby Taj

Nicknamed the Baby Taj, the exquisite **Itimad-ud-Daulah** (Indian/foreigner ₹30/310, video ₹25; ☉dawn-dusk) is the tomb of Mizra Ghiyas Beg and should not be missed. This Persian nobleman was Mumtaz Mahal's grandfather and Emperor Jehangir's *wazir* (chief minister). His daughter, Nur Jahan, built the tomb between 1622 and 1628.

It doesn't have the same awesome beauty as the Taj, but it's arguably more delicate in appearance thanks to its particularly finely carved marble *jalis* (lattice screens). This was the first Mughal structure built completely from marble, the first to make extensive use of pietra dura and the first tomb to be built on the banks of the Yamuna, which until then had been a sequence of beautiful pleasure gardens.

You can combine a trip here with Mehtab Bagh (p130), which is also on the east bank. An autorickshaw covering the two should cost about ₹500 return from the Taj, including waiting time.

they made that up). It also offers a shower and storage space (₹50 for both) to day visitors. (3/137 Chowk Kagziyan; mains ₹100-260; ⏱7am-10.30pm; 📞)

Drinking

Amarvilas Bar BAR

For a beer or cocktail in sheer opulence, look no further than the bar at Agra's best hotel (see 8 ❌ Map p128, H4). Nonguests can wander onto the terrace with its Taj views, but staff often restrict tables to in-house guests if things are busy. Bring your best shirt. (Taj East Gate Rd, Oberoi Amarvilas Hotel; beer/cocktail ₹500/950; ⏱noon-midnight)

Café Coffee Day CAFE

16 🚇 MAP P128, G4

This AC-cooled branch of the popular cafe chain right outside the Taj's east gate offers a great place to refuel after sightseeing over a proper coffee. Another branch is located at **Sadar Bazaar** (www.cafecoffeeday.com; Sadar Bazaar; coffee ₹110-135; ⏱9am-11pm). (www.cafecoffeeday.com; 21/101 Taj East Gate; coffee ₹110-135; ⏱6am-8pm)

Shopping

Subhash Emporium ARTS & CRAFTS

17 🔒 MAP P128, B5

Some of the pieces on display at this renowned marble shop are simply stunning (ask to see the 26 masterpieces). While it's more expensive than some shops, you definitely get what you pay for: high-quality marble from Rajasthan and master craftsmanship. Items for sale include tabletops, trays, lamp bases, and candle holders that glow from the flame inside. (📞9410613616; www.subhashemporium.com; 18/1 Gwalior Rd; ⏱9.30am-7pm)

Subhash Bazaar MARKET

18 🔒 MAP P128, B1

Skirts the northern edge of Agra's Jama Masjid and is particularly good for silks and saris. (⏱8am-8pm Apr-Sep, 9am-8pm Oct-Mar)

Modern Book Depot BOOKS

19 🔒 MAP P128, A6

Great selection of novels and books on Agra and the Mughals at this friendly, 60-year-old establishment. (Sadar Bazaar; ⏱10.45am-9.30pm Wed-Mon)

Worth a Trip 🔭
Fatehpur Sikri

This magnificent fortified ancient city, 40km west of Agra, was the short-lived capital of the Mughal empire between 1572 and 1585. Emperor Akbar had visited the village of Sikri to consult the Sufi saint Shaikh Salim Chishti, who predicted the birth of an heir to the Mughal throne. When the prophecy came true, Akbar built his new capital here. It was an Indo-Islamic masterpiece, but was erected in an area of water shortages, and was soon abandoned.

Indian/foreigner ₹50/610, video ₹25

🕑 dawn-dusk

Palaces & Pavilions

A large courtyard dominates the northeast entrance at **Diwan-i-Am** (Hall of Public Audiences). Now a pristinely manicured garden, this is where Akbar presided over the courts – from the middle seat of the five equal seatings along the western wall, flanked by his advisors. It was built to utilise an echo sound system, so Akbar could hear anything at anytime from anywhere in the open space. Justice was dealt with swiftly if legends are to be believed, with public executions said to have been carried out here by elephants trampling convicted criminals to death.

The **Diwan-i-Khas** (Hall of Private Audiences), found at the northern end of the Pachisi Courtyard, looks nothing special from the outside, but the interior is dominated by a magnificently carved stone central column. This pillar flares to create a futuristic flat-topped plinth linked to the four corners of the room by narrow stone bridges. From this plinth Akbar is believed to have debated with scholars and ministers who stood at the ends of the four bridges.

Next to Diwan-i-Khas is the U-shaped **Treasury**, which houses secret stone safes. Elephant-headed sea monsters carved on the ceiling struts were there to protect the fabulous wealth once stored here. The so-called **Astrologer's Kiosk** to the left has roof supports carved in a serpentine Jain style.

Just south of the Astrologer's Kiosk is **Pachisi Courtyard**, named after the ancient game known in India today as ludo. The large, plus-shaped game board is in the courtyard. In the southeast corner is the most intricately carved structure in the whole complex, the tiny but elegant **Rumi Sultana**.

Just west of the Pachisi Courtyard is the impressive **Panch Mahal**, a pavilion with five storeys that decrease in size until the top consists of only a tiny kiosk.

★ Top Tips

○ If arriving by taxi, you'll probably be dropped at the main eastern entrance near the Diwan-i-Am.

○ If coming by bus, get off at the bus stand (last stop) and climb the huge flight of stairs behind the stand to reach the Jama Masjid.

✕ Take a Break

The friendly **Hotel Ajay Palace** (☎9548801213; Agra Rd; mains ₹60-140; ⊙8am-9pm) is a convenient lunch stop near the bus stand; has rooftop seating.

★ Getting There

○ Local buses to Fatehpur Sikri (₹45, one hour, every 30 minutes, 6am to 6.30pm) leave from Idgah Bus Stand in Agra.

○ A return taxi from Agra costs at least ₹1500 for a day trip.

○ Trains for Agra leave Fatehpur Sikri at 10.14am, 3.10pm and 3.54pm. Just buy a 'general' ticket at the station (₹20, one to two hours).

Akbar's Private Quarters

Continuing anticlockwise will bring you to the **Ornamental Pool**. Here, singers and musicians would perform on the platform above the water while Akbar watched from the pavilion in his private quarters just behind, known as **Daulat Khana** (Abode of Fortune). At the back of the pavilion is the **Khwabgah** (Dream House), a sleeping area with a huge elevated stone bed platform.

Heading west through a doorway from the Ornamental Pool reveals the **Palace of Jodh Bai**, and the one-time home of Akbar's Hindu wife, said to be his favourite. Set around an enormous courtyard, it blends traditional Indian columns, Islamic cupolas and turquoise-blue Persian roof tiles. Just outside, to the left of Jodh Bai's former kitchen, is the **Palace of the Christian Wife**. This was used by Akbar's Goan wife Mariam, who gave birth to Jehangir here in 1569. Like many of the buildings in the palace complex, it contains elements of different religions, as befitted Akbar's tolerant religious beliefs. The domed ceiling is Islamic in style, while remnants of a wall painting of the Hindu god Shiva can also be found.

Jama Masjid

This beautiful, immense **mosque** (Dargah Complex; admission free) was completed in 1571. The main entrance, at the top of a flight of stone steps, is through the spectacular 54m-high **Buland Darwaza** (Victory Gate) built to commemorate Akbar's military victory in Gujarat. Inside is the stunning white marble **tomb of Sufi saint Shaikh Salim Chishti**, where women hoping to have children come to tie a thread to the *jalis* (carved lattice screens).

The saint's tomb was completed in 1581 and is entered through an original door made of ebony. Inside it are brightly coloured flower murals, while the sandalwood canopy is decorated with mother-of-pearl shell, and the marble *jalis* are among the finest in India. To the right of the tomb lie the gravestones of family members of Shaikh Salim Chishti. Just east of Shaikh Salim Chishti's tomb is the red-sandstone **tomb of Islam Khan**, the final resting place of Shaikh Salim Chishti's grandson and one-time governor of Bengal.

Guided Tours

Official Archaeological Society of India guides can be hired from the Fatehpur Sikri ticket offices at the eastern and southwestern ends of the site for ₹450 (English), but they aren't always the most knowledgeable (some are guides thanks to birthright rather than qualifications). The best guides are available in Agra, and charge ₹750. Our favourite is **Pankaj Bhatnagar** (☏8126995552; ₹750); he prefers to be messaged on WhatsApp using his phone number.

Fatehpur Sikri

0 — 200 m
0 — 0.1 miles

Chahar Suq
(Tansen Baradari)

Agra (40km)

Agra Rd

Mint

Diwan-i-Am Ticket Office &
Palace Buildings Entrance

Diwan-
i-Am

Rumi Sultana

Hammam
Astrologer's
Kiosk

Ornamental
Pool

Diwan-i-Khas
Pachisi
Courtyard

Daulat Khana
& Khwabgah

Treasury
Panch Mahal

Jodh Bai's
Kitchen

Sikri (3km)
Palace of the
Christian Wife

Jodh Bai Ticket Office &
Palace Buildings Entrance

Palace of
Jodh Bai

Hotel Ajay
Palace

Hathi
Pol

Lower
Haramsara

Bus Stand

Baoli

Birbal
Bhavan

Shahi Darwaza

Fatehpur

Tomb of
Islam Khan

Buland
Darwaza

Hiran Minar

Caravanserai

Tomb of Shaikh
Salim Chishti

Steps

Well

Jama Masjid

Stonecutters'
Mosque

Survival Guide

Indira Gandhi International Airport (p143) TOOYKRUB/SHUTTERSTOCK ©

Before You Go

Book Your Stay

○ Book ahead if you're staying in midrange or top-end accommodation, or in homestays.

○ For budget guesthouses and hotels, you'll have no problem getting rooms on the fly, and will in fact get cheaper rates as a walk-in guest.

Useful Websites

Delhi Tourism (delhi tourism.nic.in) Official tourism department website, with accommodation listings.

OYO Rooms (www. oyorooms.com) India's largest hotel network; mainly budget or lower midrange hotels.

Lonely Planet (lonely planet.com/india/delhi/ hotels) Recommendations and bookings.

Best Budget

Madpackers Hostel Only let down by its out-of-the-way location, this is Delhi's best hostel.

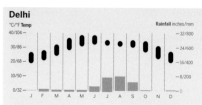

Delhi
°C/°F Temp
Rainfall inches/mm

When to Go

○ **Spring** (February–April) Sunny and pleasant, but heating up by the end of April.

○ **Summer** (May–August) The months to avoid – hot, humid and uncomfortable. July and August is monsoon season with still-high temperatures and frequent downpours.

○ **Autumn** (September–October) Pleasant time of year. Cooler following the rains, though still hot during the day.

○ **Winter** (November–January) Chilly mornings, but warm, comfortable days. Smog can ruin Delhi in November/ December, though.

GoStops (www.go stops.com) Another cool hostel, on the fringes of Old Delhi.

Backpacker Panda (www.backpackerpan da.com) Paharganj's best hostel is a little on the small side, but ideal for plugging into Delhi's traveller scene.

Tourists Rest House (www.dontworrychick encurry.com) Agra's long-standing budget favourite, with helpful owners and a pleasant central courtyard.

Hotel Kamal (hotel kamal@hotmail.com) The smartest of the cheapies in Taj Ganj, and just a stone's throw from the Taj Mahal.

Best Midrange

Diya Bed & Breakfast (http://stay.street connections.co.uk) Peaceful Old Delhi B&B with three lovely rooms, a leafy roof terrace and a family welcome.

Hotel Broadway (www. hotelbroadwaydelhi. com) Delhi's first-ever 'high-rise' hotel is a charming throwback with friendly staff and a great restaurant.

Bed & Chai (www.bedandchai.com) French-run South Delhi guesthouse with large rooms and dorms and a cute roof terrace.

Harry's Bed & Breakfast (www.harrysbedandbreakfast.com) Beautifully decorated family home with huge rooms and a quiet Gurgaon location beyond Delhi's distant suburbs.

Bansi Homestay (http://backpackerpanda.com) Wonderful upscale Agra homestay with big rooms, great food and a delightful 2nd-floor garden.

Best Top End

Haveli Dharampura (www.havelidharampura.com) A taste of Mughal India in a beautifully restored Old Delhi *haveli* (traditional courtyard home).

The Imperial (www.theimperialindia.com) Live like a king in New Delhi's sumptuous 1930s heritage hotel, just off Connaught Place.

Lutyens Bungalow (www.lutyensbungalow.co.in) Charming, family-run, Raj-era, New Delhi bungalow, with rooms set around a rambling garden.

Lodhi (www.thelodhi.com) The only hotel rooms in Delhi with their own private pools!

Oberoi Amarvilas (www.oberoihotels.com) Agra's finest luxury hotel. Immaculate throughout and with distant views of the Taj.

Arriving in Delhi & Agra

Indira Gandhi International Airport

Indira Gandhi International Airport (☎ 01243376000; www.newdelhiairport.in; Ⓜ IGI Airport) is about 14km southwest of Delhi's city centre.

Metro The Airport Express line (5.15am to 11.40pm, every 10 mins) runs from Terminal 3 to New Delhi train station (30 minutes).

Bus Air-conditioned buses run from outside Terminal 3 to Kashmere Gate ISBT (Delhi's main bus station) every 10 minutes, via the Red Fort, LNJP Hospital, New Delhi Station Gate 2, Connaught Place, Parliament St and Ashoka Rd.

Taxi In front of the arrivals buildings are Delhi Traffic Police Prepaid Taxi counters offering fixed-price taxi services. Most hotels offer prearranged airport pick-up, though this will work out more expensive.

New Delhi Railway Station

o The largest and best connected of Delhi's train stations.

o Has its own metro station with a direct line to the airport.

o Houses the very helpful **International Tourist Bureau** (ITB; Map p62, D1; ☎ 011-23405156; 1st fl, New Delhi Train Station; ⊙6am-10pm; Ⓜ New Delhi), a ticket office reserved solely for the use of foreign travellers (inside the main entrance, and up on the first floor; don't believe anyone who tells you it's closed).

○ The 6.45am Taj Express (three hours to Agra) leaves from here.

Agra Cantonment (Cantt) train station

Trains Early-morning express trains are well set up for day trippers from Delhi, but trains run to/from Delhi all day, taking three to four hours.

Taxi/autorickshaw For fixed-price fares into town, there are prepaid taxi and autorickshaw booths outside the station. Most hotels can arrange a train-station pick-up.

Getting Around

Metro

○ Fast and efficient, with signs and arrival/departure announcements in Hindi and English.

○ Trains run from around 6am to 11pm.

○ First carriage in the direction of travel is reserved for women only.

○ Single-trip tokens (₹10 to ₹60) are sold at metro stations.

○ A smart card (₹50 deposit plus ₹100 minimum initial top-up) gets you 10% off all journeys (20% outside the peak hours of 8am to noon and 5pm to 9pm).

○ There's no metro in Agra.

Autorickshaw

○ Delhi's signature green-and-yellow autorickshaws are everywhere (in Agra too).

○ You never have to worry about finding one – drivers will find you!

○ They have meters, but they are never used, so negotiate the fare clearly before you start your journey.

○ At train stations there are fixed-price autorickshaw booths.

E-rickshaw

○ Delhi's ever-expanding fleet of golf-cart-lookalike e-rickshaws (electric rickshaws)

offer a more environmentally friendly alternative to autorickshaws and taxis.

○ Many of them are shared vehicles, plying fixed routes for very cheap individual fares, but some can also be hired privately.

○ Private fares are roughly the same as autorickshaws.

Cycle rickshaw

○ Great fun for navigating Old Delhi, the outer suburbs and Agra, but they are banned from some parts of New Delhi, including Connaught Place.

○ Negotiate a fare before you set off – expect to pay ₹20 to ₹30 for a short trip.

○ Tip well; it's a tough job, and many rickshaw riders are homeless and spend the nights sleeping on their rickshaws.

Taxi

○ As with autorickshaws, taxi meters are largely ornamental; negotiate the fare beforehand.

○ Train stations and the airport have fixed-price taxi ranks.

o Taxi apps (Uber and Ola Cabs) are beginning to supersede ordinary taxis. They're cheaper, but usually take longer, including all the faff involved with them trying to find you.

Essential Information

Accessible Travel

Accessibility Some restaurants and offices have ramps but most tend to have at least one step. Staircases are often quite steep; lifts frequently stop at mezzanines between floors.

Accommodation Wheelchair-friendly hotels are almost exclusively top-end. Make enquiries before travelling and book ground-floor rooms at hotels that lack adequate facilities.

Footpaths Pavements in Delhi and Agra can be riddled with holes, littered with debris and crowded. If using crutches, bring along spare rubber caps.

Transport Hiring a car with driver will make moving around a lot easier; if you use a wheelchair, make sure the car-hire company can provide an appropriate vehicle.

Business Hours

Banks 10am to 4pm Monday to Friday, 10am to 1pm Saturday

Restaurants 8am or 9am to 11pm or midnight (some midrange and top-end restaurants may not open till lunchtime; some restaurants close between 3pm and 7pm; some stay open as late as 1.30am)

Bars noon to 12.30am

Shops 10am or 11am to 8pm or 9pm (some close later)

Sights 9am or 10am to 5pm or 6pm; many close on Mondays; parks and temples are often open either 24 hours or from dawn to dusk

Dos & Don'ts

Dress modestly Avoid offence by not wearing tight, sheer and skimpy clothes.

Shoes It's polite to remove shoes before entering homes and places of worship.

Photos Best to ask before snapping people, sacred sites or ceremonies. Photography is not allowed inside some places of worship. You have to pay ₹300 for the privilege at Delhi's Jama Masjid.

Bad vibes Avoid pointing soles of feet towards people or deities, or touching anyone with your feet.

Hello Saying *namaste* with hands together in a prayer gesture is a respectful Hindu greeting; for Muslims say *salaam alaikum* ('peace be with you'; response: *alaikum salaam*).

Head wobble Can mean 'yes', 'no', or 'I have no idea'.

Pure touch The right hand is for eating and shaking hands, the left is the 'toilet' hand.

Electricity

Type C
220V/50Hz

Type M
230V/50Hz

Type D
220V/50Hz

Emergency & Important Numbers

India's country code	☎ 91
International access code	☎ 00
Ambulance	☎ 112
Fire	☎ 112
Police	☎ 112

Internet Access

○ Pretty much all accommodation and most cafes, bars and restaurants offer free wi-fi access these days.

○ There are some free wi-fi hotspots around Delhi, in some shopping malls, for example, and in airport buildings.

○ Internet cafes are a thing of the past.

○ It's easy to gain 3G and 4G access via smartphone data packs bought for local SIM cards.

LGBT Travellers

○ Despite a landmark decision by India's Supreme Court in 2018, which ruled that gay sex in India was no longer a criminal offence, India's LGBT+ scene remains relatively discreet, though less so in cities such as Delhi.

○ The capital hosts the annual Queer Pride (www.facebook.com/delhiqueerpride) in November.

○ Delhi also has a men-only gay guesthouse, Mister & Art House (www.misterandarthouse.com), in South Delhi, which is run by Delhi-based gay travel agency Indjapink (www.indjapink.co.in), who also offer tailor-made tours.

○ Serene Journeys (www.serenejourneys.co) is also recommended as a gay-friendly travel agency.

Money

ATMs & Card Payments

o ATMs are everywhere, especially in Delhi.

o Cards are accepted at many hotels, shops and restaurants, but you'll still need to have local currency for many transactions.

Bargaining

Except in fixed-price shops (such as government emporiums and fair-trade co-operatives), bargaining is the norm. Remember to keep a sense of perspective, though, and always barter in good humour.

Tipping

Restaurants A service fee is often added to your bill at restaurants and hotels. Elsewhere a tip is appreciated; 10% is about right.

Hotels If you're staying in high-end hotels, bellboys and the like will expect tips.

Transport Train or airport porters will expect tips, but not taxi or auto drivers. Tipping cycle-rickshaw riders is

good form given the job they do. If you hire a car with driver, tip for good service.

Safe Travel

o Delhi and Agra are relatively safe in terms of petty crime, though pickpocketing can be a problem in crowded areas so keep your valuables safe.

o Roads are notoriously congested; take extreme care when crossing them, or when walking along narrow lanes which don't have pavements.

o Pollution is another real danger, particularly in Delhi. Consider wearing a properly-fitting face mask.

o Women should never walk in lonely, deserted places, even during daylight hours.

o Be aware of touts at airports, train stations and around tourist areas.

o Beware of fake tourist offices, particularly around Delhi's Connaught Place.

Smoking

o The 2008 ban on smoking in public places

in India is generally well enforced in Delhi, although some of the very cheapest guesthouses may smell smoky, so check your room before committing.

o You can smoke in restaurants with terraces or gardens.

o Sadly, smoking is on the rise in India, although *paan* (chewing tobacco) is still more popular.

Telephone Services

o You can use your unlocked mobile phone from home on roaming, but it's much cheaper to buy a local SIM card.

o You'll need your passport to register a local SIM, and the details of your accommodation.

o It's best to buy a local SIM card with a data package either from the airport when you arrive, or from a genuine branch of one of the main phone providers in the city centre; **Vodafone** (Map p62, D2; D27, Connaught Place; ⏰10.30am-7.30pm Mon-Sat; Ⓜ Rajiv Chowk) or **Airtel** (Map p62, D3; No 5 M-Block, Radial Rd 5,

Connaught Place; 10am-8pm Mon-Sat; **M** Rajiv Chowk) are the most reliable. If you go through a local shop or kiosk you may experience delays in getting connected, or be overcharged.

Toilets

○ There are numerous public toilets dotted around Delhi, especially in Old Delhi and the more heavily populated areas.

○ Most modern public toilets, in places such as shopping malls, have a sit-down toilet as well as squat toilets, but in older facilities, there will only be squat toilets.

○ Sometimes you are expected to pay a few rupees to a toilet attendant, though this is becoming increasingly rare.

○ Some of the newer metro stations have public toilets.

○ Toilet paper is almost never provided in public toilets (always carry tissues with you, or use the bidet system), and soap is rarely available (travel hand wash is useful).

○ Some low-budget guesthouses may only have squat toilets, but most accommodation now has sit-down toilets in en-suite bathrooms.

Tourist Information

India Tourism, Delhi

(Government of India; Map p62, D3; 011-23320008, 011-23320005; www. incredibleindia.org; 88 Janpath; 9am-6pm Mon-Fri, to 2pm Sat; **M** Janpath) This official tourist office is a useful source of advice on Delhi, getting out of Delhi, and visiting surrounding states. But note, this is the only official tourist information centre outside the airport. Ignore touts who (falsely) claim to be associated with this office. Anyone who 'helpfully' approaches you is definitely not going to take you to the real office.

India Tourism, Agra

(Map p128, A5; 0562-2226378; www.incredible india.org; 191 The Mall; 9am-5.30pm Mon-Fri) Helpful branch; has brochures on local and India-wide attractions.

UP Tourism, Agra

(0562-2421204; www. up-tourism.com; Agra Cantonment Train Station; 6.30am-9.30pm) The friendly train-station branch inside the Tourist Facilitation Centre on Platform 1 offers helpful advice and is where you can book day-long bus tours of Agra. This branch doubles as the Tourist Police.

Visas

Most nationals can stay in India for up to 60 days with a hassle-free, double-entry, e-Visa (www. indianvisaonline.gov. in/evisa). Longer stays (up to six months) require a standard tourist visa.

Language

Hindi

Hindi has about 600 million speakers worldwide, of which 180 million are in India. It developed from Classical Sanskrit, and is written in the Devanagari script. In 1947 it was granted official status along with English.

Most Hindi sounds are similar to their English counterparts. The main difference is that Hindi has both 'aspirated' consonants (pronounced with a puff of air, like saying 'h' after the sound) and unaspirated ones, as well as 'retroflex' (pronounced with the tongue bent backwards) and nonretroflex consonants. Our simplified pronunciation guides don't include these distinctions – read them as if they were English and you'll be understood.

Pronouncing the vowels correctly is important, especially their length (eg *a* and *aa*). The consonant combination *ng* after a vowel indicates nasalisation (ie the vowel is pronounced 'through the nose'). Note also that *au* is pronounced as the 'ow' in 'how'. Word stress is very light – we've indicated the stressed syllables with italics.

Hindi verbs change form depending on the gender of the speaker (or the subject of the sentence in general), so it's the verbs, not the pronouns 'he' or 'she' (as is the case in English) which show whether the subject of the sentence is masculine or feminine. In these phrases we include the options for male and female speakers, marked 'm' and 'f' respectively.

Basics

Hello./Goodbye.
नमस्ते ।   na·ma·*ste*

Yes.
जी हाँ ।   jee haang

No.
जी नहीं ।   jee na·*heeng*

Excuse me.
सुनिये ।   su·ni·*ye*

Sorry.
माफ़ कीजिये ।   maaf *kee*·ji·ye

Please ...
कृपया …   kri·pa·*yaa* ...

Thank you.
थैंक्यू ।   *thayn*·kyoo

How are you?
आप कैसे/कैसी हैं ?
aap *kay*·se/*kay*·see hayng (m/f)

Fine. And you?
मैं ठीक हूँ । आप सुनाइये ।
mayng teek hoong aap su·*naa*·i·ye

Do you speak English?
क्या आपको अंग्रेज़ी आती है ?
kyaa aap ko an·*gre*·zee *aa*·tee hay

How much is this?
कितने का है ?
kit·ne kaa hay

I don't understand.
मैं नहीं समझा/समझी ।
mayng na·*heeng sam*·jaa/
sam·jee (m/f)

Accommodation

Do you have a single/double room?
क्या सिंगल/डबल कमरा है?
kyaa sin·gal/da·bal kam·raa hay

How much is it (per night/per person)?
(एक रात/हर व्यक्ति) के लिये कितने पैसे लगते हैं?
(ek raat/har vyak·ti) ke li·ye kit·ne
pay·se lag·te hayng

Eating & Drinking

I'd like ..., please.
मुझे ... दीजिये ।
mu·je ... dee·ji·ye

That was delicious.
बहुत मज़ेदार हुआ ।
ba·hut ma·ze·daar hu·aa

Please bring the menu/bill.
मेन्यू/बिल लाइये ।
men·yoo/bil laa·i·ye

I don't eat ...
मैं ... नहीं खाता/खाती ।
mayng ... na·heeng·kaa·taa/
kaa·tee (m/f)

fish	मछली	mach·lee
meat	गोश्त	gosht
poultry	मुर्गी	mur·gee

Emergencies

I'm ill.
मैं बीमार हूँ ।
mayng bee·maar hoong

Help!
मदद कीजिये!
ma·dad kee·ji·ye

Call the doctor/police!
डॉक्टर/पुलिस को बुलाओ!
daak·tar/pu·lis ko bu·laa·o

Directions

Where's a/the ...?
... कहाँ है? ... ka·haang hay

bank
बैंक baynk

market
बाज़ार baa·zaar

post office
डाक ख़ाना daak kaa·naa

restaurant
रेस्टोरेंट res·to·rent

toilet
टॉइलेट taa·i·let

tourist office
पर्यटन ऑफ़िस
par·ya·tan·aa·fis

To enhance your trip with a phrasebook, visit lonelyplanet.com.

Behind the Scenes

Send Us Your Feedback

We love to hear from travellers – your comments help make our books better. We read every word, and we guarantee that your feedback goes straight to the authors. Visit **lonelyplanet.com/contact** to submit your updates and suggestions.

Note: We may edit, reproduce and incorporate your comments in Lonely Planet products such as guidebooks, websites and digital products, so let us know if you don't want your comments reproduced or your name acknowledged. For a copy of our privacy policy visit lonelyplanet.com/privacy.

Daniel's Thanks

In Delhi, a warm *namaste* to my friends at Diya B&B – Pradeep, Mr B, Pash, Catriona, Paula – and an especially huge thanks to Nick, and to Dilip and his beautiful family, for being such wonderful hosts. At LP, huge thanks to Joe for trusting in me, to Bradley and Abi for all your expert help, and to Martine, Anne and Dianne for solving my seemingly endless list of technical queries. Back home, much love, hugs and kisses to Taotao and our two incredible children, Yoyo and Dudu.

Bradley's Thanks

Thanks to Rouf in Rinagar; Anil and Ramesh Wadhwa in Agra; Zaheer Bagh in Kargil; Juma Malik and Tashi of Hidden North in Leh; Harish and Michael Schmid in Varanasi. Thanks to Carolyn for keeping me company in Varanasi.

Acknowledgements

Cover photograph: Diwan-i-Am, Red Fort, Nigel Pavitt/AWL Images ©

This Book

This 1st edition of Lonely Planet's *Pocket Delhi & Agra* guidebook was curated, researched and written by Daniel McCrohan. The Agra section was researched and written by Bradley Mayhew. This guidebook was produced by the following:

Destination Editor
Joe Bindloss

Senior Product Editors
Kate Chapman, Anne Mason, Martine Power

Regional Senior Cartographer Valentina Kremenchutskaya

Product Editor
Katie Connolly

Book Designer
Mazzy Prinsep

Cover Researcher
Naomi Parker

Thanks to Carolyn Boicos, Sasha Drew, Victoria Harrison, Kate Kiely, Wayne Murphy, Jessica Rose, Wibowo Rusli, Julie Sheridan, Vicky Smith, Diana Von Holdt

Index

See also separate subindexes for:

⊗ **Eating p155**

◉ **Drinking p155**

✪ **Entertainment p155**

🔒 **Shopping p156**

Sights 000
Map Pages **000**

😣 Eating

A

Agarwal Chat House 133
Agra Chat House 132, 133
Al-Jawahar 50
Altitude Cafe & Deli 87
Ama 50
Andhra Pradesh Bhawan Canteen 67

B

Bade Mia Ki Kheer 41, 47-8
Basil & Thyme 87-8
Big Chill Cafe 103
Bikaner Sweet Corner 51
Burma Burma 117

C

Cafe Lota 67-8
Cafe Red 102
Chor Bizarre 50
Coast 102
Coffee Home 69
Cyber Hub Social 116, 117

D

Darbar 48
Dasaprakash 133
Diva 117
Diva Spiced 88
DLF Cyber Hub 117
Dolma House 50

E

Epicuria 103
Esphahan 132
Evergreen 103

F

Farzi Cafe 117

G

Gujarat Bhawan 86

H

Hotel Saravana Bhavan 67

I

Immigrant Cafe 88
Indian Accent 85

J

Jalebi Wala 41, 47
Joney's Place 134

K

Kake-da-Hotel 68-9
Karim's 46, 86-7
Kebab Stands 87
Kheer 116
Krishna Cafe 51

L

Lakhori 48

M

Madhuban 115
Mama Chicken 131
Mamagoto 85
Mughal Room 133

N

Nagaland House 86
Naivedyam 101
National Museum cafe 59

Natraj Dahi Balle Corner 46
Naturals 69

O

Olive 117

P

Perch 86, 88
Pinch of Spice 132-3
Potbelly 102, 105
PT Gaya Prasad Shiv Charan 41, 47

R

Rose Cafe 116

S

Sagar Ratna 88-9
Saniya Palace Hotel 133
Satguru Dhaba 51
Shankara Vegis 134
Shim Tur 51
Sita Ram Dewan Chand 48-9
Sodabottleopenerwala 86, 88

T

Tadka 49
Tee Dee 50
Triveni Terrace Cafe 68

V

Véda 68

Y

Yash Cafe 134-5

🍷 Drinking

1911 69
Amarvilas Bar 135

Atrium 61, 70
Big Chill 88, 89
Blue Tokai 117
Cafe Brownie 52
Café Coffee Day 135
Café Turtle 88, 89
Cha Bar 70
Chai Point 70
Diggin Cafe 90
Ek Bar 104
Hauz Khas Social 97, 103-4
Hotel Aiwan-e-Shahi Rooftop Cafe 52
Indian Coffee House 70
Jugmug Thela 118
Keventer's Milkshakes 71
Kunzum Travel Cafe 97, 104
Latitude 28° 90
Lord of the Drinks 71
Madras Coffee House 117
Piano Man Jazz Club 103
PT Ved Prakash Lemon Wale 51
Sam's Bar 52
Soi 7 117, 118
Summer House Cafe 104
Unplugged 70
Voyage Cafe 52

🎭 Entertainment

Akshara Theatre 71
Delite Cinema 52
Habitat World 90
India International Centre 90-1
Indira Gandhi National Centre for the Arts 71

Sights **000**
Map Pages **000**